Y0-BSC-668

THE QUIET REBELLION

JAMES K. FEIBLEMAN

BY THE SAME AUTHOR
Aesthetics
In Praise of Comedy
The Way of a Man, an autobiography
Great April, a novel

THE QUIET REBELLION

the Making and Meaning of the Arts

HORIZON PRESS   NEW YORK

Preface

Man does not give the world its values, he finds them there. He himself is a product of that world and native to it; he manages to survive in it by adapting to it. One form of his adaptation consists in the production of works of art. The material environment contains everything, including aspects of beauty which man needs very badly to have disclosed. This is the special task of the artist, who functions as a sensitive recording mechanism. By means of art the artist engineers a quiet rebellion which liberates us from the tyranny of our times, and enables us to glimpse that cosmic sublimity which lies above the more hostile aspects of our existence.

In the following chapters I have tried to put my readers in touch with the artist's perspective and to give some concrete examples. A few of these chapters first appeared as journal articles: "Artistic Imagining" in *The Personalist*, Vol. 46 (1965); "Artistical Resemblances" in *The Journal of Aesthetic Education*, Vol. 4, No. 3 (1970); "A Behaviorist Theory of Art" in *The British Journal of Aesthetics*, Vol. 3 (1963); "Concreteness in Painting" in *The Personalist*, Vol. 42 (1962); "The Art of the Philosophy of Art" in *Tulane Studies in Philosophy*, Vol. XIX (1970); "Art: A Definition and Some Consequences" in *The Personalist*, Vol. 48 (1967); "The Truth-Value of Art" in *The Journal of Aesthetics and Art Criticism*, XXIV (1966); "The Criticism of Art" in the *Revue d' Esthetique*, Vol. XX (1967); "On The Metaphysics of the Performing Arts" in the *Journal of Aesthetics and Art Criticism*, Vol. XXVIII (1970); and finally "Bad Art" in *Tulane Studies in Philosophy*, Vol. XX (1971), to whose editors acknowledgment is due.

Tulane University
September 1971

Contents

PART ONE

Method

ONE
Artistic Imagining

The activity of image-making is not confined to artists but is a common one and its prevalence can hardly be doubted. We know about it from our own experience as well as from the description furnished us by others. It will help us to understand artistic imagining if we approach it through some of its ramified associations with non-artistic functions as well as directly. Imagining belongs to the ordinary behavior of all men; it gives shape to dreams; it is built into the scientific method; and it is a necessary part of the equipment of those who guide practical affairs. The identification given to the reference of the term by all of the various activities in which it participates confronts us with an isolable fact. Since we can hardly dismiss imagining as something too removed for technical consideration, we must therefore set out to learn what we can even if we do not solve all of the puzzles connected with it.

METHOD

Imagining as a function plays a role in events, and as a process is the qualitative side of the experience of the individual. But as a function it cannot be directly observed, and as a qualitative process it cannot be analyzed. Those who have demonstrated that they possess a strong imagination argue that they did not acquire it through learning, and we know from the many unsuccessful attempts that it cannot be taught.

Perhaps the best approach to image-making will be from the biological sciences, more particularly from behavioristic psychology and physiology.

In the human individual, there is sometimes said to be only one generalized need: to dominate the environment by means of aggression. All other needs are considered specialized subdivisions. Each need exemplifies the character of the generalized need by the peculiar way in which the individual endeavors to dominate his environment. He strives to compel it to include him by seeking in it for just those elements which will further his immediate survival, such as water, food and a mate, and for just those secondary elements which will assure his continued survival, such as knowledge, activity and security. The activation of a need is a drive, and the consummatory response results in drive-reduction and the restoration of equilibrium.

The generic need has its own peculiar properties: the need to be counted part of the largest possible environment by means of intimate connections, the more passive need for an integrated world in which a disparately engaged and partially unrelated animal organism can find a hospitable niche. The need for aggression is the need to dominate the world as a *whole*. The need to be counted a *part* is the need to be included *by* the whole. The former involves primarily activity; the latter, primarily feeling. Not just any feelings are involved but specifically those four stages involving learning, retention, recall and recognition of images.

The learned material consists in the content of sensations, the elementary awareness of stimuli without any further interpretation than was involved in their selection: stimulations, of relatively short duration, of the central nervous system recognizable as images, patterns of qualities which will stand for previous experience.

Retention consists in the capacity to store patterns of qualities in such a way that they are available for reproduction, stimuli to which the response is delayed. Retention, in other words, means a response reserve in which the pattern prevails over the qualities.

Recall means the capacity to evoke learned material so that it once again occupies the position of stimuli. Recall is a restoration in which, however, there has been a turn-over so that the qualities prevail over the pattern.

It is in the last of the four stages, that of recognition, that the property of imagining makes its first appearance. Recognition is the identification of images as the stimuli of previous responses. Here, however, there is the added function of response generalization. The connections between the images and the previous stimuli are so much stronger than either the images or the previous stimuli that they are carried over to similar images which were retained from other stimuli lying along the same stimulus continuum. Such similarities have their own powerful qualities which are bound to them by the images they connect. The flow of images exceeds in quality either of the separate component images. Now the qualities and the pattern are in equilibrium for the first time.

METHOD

Evidently the background required is one involving extra pyramidal control of the autonomic nervous system. The contents constitute the matrix and in a certain sense furnish the cues. The process begins with the prospect of matching. A high state of arousal is necessary to facilitate the connections between remote phenomena. The impulses have a long way to travel, and they will be made only if they are compelled to move quickly, only, that is, if the pathways are open and the extra energy supplied. In a closed pathway it is possible to make circular connections. The specific response made to the similarity between naturally occurring relations is reinforced by the patterning of qualities in matched images. For in the process the two images are brought together in a way in which they were not together in the original sensations so that now their similarities can be observed. This is the preparatory response. Imagining itself is the consummatory response reducing the generalized drive state.

The obvious distinction which first occurs to those who direct their interest at imagining separates it into the uncontrolled and the controlled varieties. I will consider uncontrolled imagining first, and secondly the controlled variety. Artistic imagining, with which I am chiefly concerned here, is controlled, but something can be learned from the contrast.

Uncontrolled imagining is involuntary in the human individual. Involuntary recall may have with it that element of selection which amounts to a weak act of imagining. Uncontrolled imagining may result in emotional gratifications and bring with it all sorts of need-reductions. A familiar example is that of the daydream. Something which could not ordinarily happen is contemplated in an evoked image. The daydream may for instance serve to reduce tension. It may be a form of relaxation or play, or it may be a form of substitution, as for instance when a man ordinarily timid imagines that he is masterful or successful.

Another version of the uncontrolled dream is the dream of sleep. In the dream, elements of experience are reassembled in fresh ways which disclose the operation of imagining. Freud thought that an unconscious motivation gave the dream an effectiveness in waking life. He thought that it served forbidden wishes, which, although banished to the unconscious, continued to influence behavior, but could be siphoned off harmlessly in this way. Dreams, then, release repressed desires: they are hidden wish-fulfillments.

Uncontrolled imagining is by itself usually unproductive of any permanent effects; there are by ordinary standards no constructive material results. No one by its means alone has ever painted pictures or constructed blueprints for an ideal society. Yet dreams do have their constructive side. A wish need not always be a forbidden fulfillment. It may merely be an impractical one. It is not forbidden to me to found a university; I have no hidden feelings of guilt about the desire. I simply lack the cash and perhaps by now the energy. However, I solve some of the problems in dreams, and should there be a financial windfall I am prepared. For I have in this way imagined how an academic institution ought to function.

It is a mistake, however, to think of the dream of sleep entirely in emotional terms. In the *Republic* (571 C) Plato argued that in dreams there is a release from reason, but what he mistook for the absence of reason was the presence of another sort of reason, for "the wild beast within us" has his own laws. In existence, there is always some logic in operation, although there is more than one sort of logic. The logic of dreams differs from ordinary logic. In dreams, for instance, identity is represented by equivalence. If similarity is partial identity, then in the dream it is possible to substitute partial equivalence. Where dreams relate situations which in the waking state are conventionally disparate, through the substitution of equivalence for identity it is no longer necessary for the images to be so sharply defined but relatedness can be achieved through similarity. In dream situations where partial equivalence has actually been employed, emotive elements are found replacing prescriptive ones. Identity carries the similarity as a weak form in ordinary logic, whereas in dream logic a preference is indicated. For instance, the night after an author received a letter of rejection for a book he had submitted to a publisher he dreamed that he was prevented from having a love affair with the wife of a neighbor by the friend who had in fact mailed the manuscript.

There is a logic to dreams in many respects unlike that of actual life. The impossible events which happen in dreams have in fact their own type of consistency. One characteristic of dream logic is that in dreams pieces of experience are fitted together without regard to their temporal sequence or spatial juxtaposition. What seems from the point of view of the dream to belong together is put together, and actions are assembled which never could otherwise have occurred. Thus dream logic is a kind of intentional logic: it brings together what is important to the dreamer to have together, and then considers them as events.

Thus while I have used dreams as a familiar example of uncontrolled imagining, the existence of a dream logic shows that it is not altogether random and chaotic. What is uncontrolled is not necessarily for that reason altogether lacking in order. Uncontrolled imagining has its own type of order just as, we shall presently note, controlled imagining has its own type of disorder. It should not be forgotten that a dream is to some extent at least a construction. A dream is in fact a work similar to the work of art, but unplanned, uncontrolled, and lacking the permanence or force, and hence the great beauty, of art. Art logic can be studied in dreams because of its similarity to dream logic. What ought to be together for qualitative reasons is brought together through the emotions which represent the qualities psychologically.

I shall not concern myself with these uncontrolled types of dreams except as they contribute to the understanding of the controlled type. The distinction between unproductive and productive imagaining is not nearly so sharp as I have been describing it. Properly speaking, uncontrolled imagining may be in some instances a subclass of controlled imagining. Autistic thinking may as a matter of fact have its incidental productive aspect. It brings together all of the elements which go into making up an imaginary world by uniting them at one end with the self as a focus. Thus it foreshadows productive thinking which often begins in the same way and manages to be productive simply because it does not stop there but goes on with the process until something useful results. My concern in this study is chiefly with the productive and controlled variety.

I define "controlled imagining" as "that deliberate exercise in which the elements disclosed to experience are broken up and reassembled under the conditions promoted by a high state of arousal."

Controlled imagining is what is meant by the ordinary

use of the term, "imagination": it functions to offer images as alternatives to facts. Since controlled imagining is a voluntary act, it has an aim: the reconstruction of some segment of the world through images in order to make a contrast with the method of planning or substituting for need-reductions. Thus acts of imagining may be either planned realities later to be carried out or substitute realities calling for no further action because they are themselves need-reductions.

The practical man of action is concerned with planning for need-reductions, imagining how things could be after interference as contrasted with how they will be without interference. If the environment has to be rearranged in order to provide the proper consummatory acts, the practical man can test this eventuality in advance by means of pictures in a preparatory act of imagining.

The theoretical man of contemplation is concerned with substituting for future need-reductions; imagining how things ought to be as contrasted with how they are likely to be. In this way the possibilities can be compared and contrasted; unattainable goals become prospectively attainable, and additional varieties of adaptation envisaged.

These are anticipations; there is also the substitution of the dreamer: imagining how things could be as its own need-reduction, including reward and reinforcement on successive occasions of imagining. The individual here takes delight in his own constructions. The unpopular youth may imagine himself a Prince Charming and in this way enjoy a projected personality.

Once we recognize the phenomemon of controlled imagining it is easy to understand that it admits of presuppositions. All formal structures have their axioms, and although this is conventionally recognized only in logical systems, it is equally true of deliberate activities. The starting assumptions or first principles of controlled imagining are no less strong and operative because implicit and unacknowledged.

Among the assumptions made by imagining when controlled are: (*a*) that all things are related affectively by means of their qualities; (*b*) that these relations can be shown in such a way that the feelings respond to them; and (*c*) that (therefore) the feelings can be a source of knowledge.

(*a*) The assumption that all things are related by means of their qualities underlies all acts of imagining. In any imaginative occasion chosen at random there is a disclosure of similarity among differences, with the similarity qualitatively presented. This can best be shown if a similarity can be found between two elements chosen especially for the radical nature of their differences. The two elements involved in the comparison will have to be selected so that they are at a great distance from each other in space and time, and they should also if possible be chosen so that they are at a logical distance also.

The nature of imagining can best be seen by contrasting the aspects selected by science and art. Science is concerned with the laws of relatedness of objects in relative spatial and temporal connection, the relatedness of sun and planets for instance or of electron and nucleus in the hydrogen atom. Here the underlying qualities are those of physical forces. Art is more concerned to bring together and relate the images of disparate as well as absent objects. When the news arrives of Antony's death, Caesar says, "We could not stall together in the whole world." Here the qualities are those of the stable: the smells and sounds of horses but very much magnified.

In the older associationism dating from Aristotle but continuing with Hume, similarity, contrast and contiguity were the relations selected as the significant ones. But contiguity can be construed as a kind of similarity in time and space; it will be necessary to add now also contrast or difference in time and space, and this is supplied by the relation of remoteness, as we can see from the last example, "We could not stall together in the whole world."

Our task is to seek an explanation of why quality emerges from the connections of objects which are widely-spaced. Controlled imagining, insofar as it is imagining at all, has a wild side. This feature is of the essence of imagining, for it is only by ranging into the improbable that one encounters the unforeseen and the valuable. But this can be done in quite familiar ways. We are able to witness such phenomena not only in works of art but in the ordinary business of everyday life, like the custom in Oklahoma of setting out fence posts at night by the North Star.

The older association psychology was given up too quickly and completely. It has relevance to the analysis of the act of imaginative discovery. To imagine what there could be, a man has first to learn something of what there is. A wealth of experience, keen powers of observation, and a tremendous memory for details, are all part of the equipment, but in the final summing, similarities and differences can be found only within knowledge. A man who had sailed with Joseph Conrad in his early years in southeast Asia was struck with the abundance of minute detail dealing with that period of his life which Conrad had remembered and used in his novels. The more a man knows, the more he is able to associate.

(*b*) Imagining brings together naturally occurring objects or their properties that either do not or could not come together in the absence of human agency. Exactly how does this work? Sense images are recalled and recombined in new structures so that they can provide new experiences. What the man did who first imagined a unicorn was to bring together before his experience the horn of a rhinoceros and the body of a horse, but thenceforth he as well as others responded to it as a to a new image, which it certainly was. The first unicorn was completely available for covering with affects by imagining them. It had no traditional associations and so fresh ones could be assigned to it through context. The unicorn is a new entity made up of old relations and is charged with the associations given it in the earliest accounts of its behavior.

Such artificial objects are composed of the elements of naturally occurring objects, only reassembled in a way which presents the qualities uppermost. The essence of imagining is image-making, whether metaphor or myth, by means of a grasping into unity of disparate and least likely comparisons. It is an abstraction but with content, and composed in a way which is most affective. The unicorn has a new identity, and one moreover which is provocative of feeling. Thus images produced by the mind out of the material available through recall furnish the raw data for thoughts, feelings and even actions which might otherwise not have been possible, or where possible might not have occurred. Imagining brings together disparate elements in such a way as to increase the order in the world and thus represents a lawful force. The controlled image is a description with respect to feelings, thoughts and actions in favor of an increase in order.

(*c*) What kind of knowledge do we derive from the feelings? A knowledge of the unity of the universe and of how it can be intuited through the qualities. The strength of such unity could be neither observed nor ascertained from the outside, from which perspective, presumably, it would appear only as a whole. But some evidence for it can be observed from the inside where it is structured of internal relations, the relations between lesser wholes. Thus we are able to feel the bonds between material objects as values, while under the aspect of the universe they would still be relations. Now some things occur together always while others come together occasionally, yet both may be naturally occurring events taking place in the absence of human agency. Still others are brought together routinely as a result of the ordinary behavior of the human animal. But there are certain possibilities which would not ordinarily be actualized in any of these ways. Such possibilities are actualized as the result of deliberate acts of imagining.

Let us see how this works in actual practice. Art will furnish us with our most graphic example. The artist tries to imagine what-ought-to-be against the very specific background of what-is. Let us consider for example the act of imagining as it occurs in the familiar literary device of the trope. By pointing to the similarity of two objects, one small and one large, a logical bridge is built, so that over it there can take place a transfer of feeling from the large to the small, thus accomplishing the supercharging of the small. A man who is in love with a beautiful woman sees a pool fringed with lilies. He is at once struck with the similarity of shape between the eyelash-fringed eyes of his beloved and the lily-fringed pool. The pool is a much larger object than the eyes, but the eyes have an equal beauty, indicated by the flow of value from the former to the latter.

The effects of lyric poems and of the plastic arts, such as painting and sculpture, are like this. But a flow of feeling from the larger to the smaller occurs in another way in the temporal arts, such as music, the theatre or the novel. Here the effect is not instantaneous but cumulative; the feeling does not flow from the larger to the smaller but from the earlier to the later. It becomes bunched toward the end of the work of art which requires time for its exposition as the intensity and depth of the structure makes itself increasingly evident.

It is reassuring to feel the relatedness of things in time, probably because, since we too are things, the relatedness of things includes us. In this way each time we hear an imagined comparison it confirms us in our hope that we have somehow a permanent place in the world. We are authentic parts of the world if all things are, and this is comforting. The feeling of belonging is a good feeling; because of it we are no longer isolated or alien.

If the unity of the universe is one kind of knowledge acquired through the feelings by the process of imagining, lawfulness is another. Order consists in elements conforming to regulative principles, and this after all is what we mean by law: general conditions to which no observed exceptions have been reported. Again, works of art will prove illustrative. One variety of artistic product is attained either by breaking up the ordinary elements of order to show another and more subtle order beneath, or by showing in the least orderly of arrangements that there is still an order. The various geometric configurations prevalent in painting since Cézanne, such as pointillism and cubism, show the lawfulness of colored shapes. Dadaism and abstract expressionism are varieties of the second method.

For every quality there is a corresponding relation, as for instance the wave-lengths of color; but also for every relation there is a corresponding quality. By exchanging the relations with which we are too familiar for others, the quality of the unfamiliar is driven forcefully home. For it is as Bacon said, "there is no great art that hath not some strangeness in the proportions."

The attempt to explain imagining may now be taken into some of the various institutional forms of human behavior in order to show what roles it plays and what are the consequences of its assumptions in theory and practice. We are interested chiefly in understanding artistic imagining, but imagining is equally a function in technology, in science, and in the practical life generally. It will help us to understand artistic imagining if we glance at these other forms of imagining first.

In the technique of invention, the individual imagines how materials in his immediate environment could be rearranged so as to provide the tools requisite for making a preparatory response to a need. In advance of the construction of every artifact—a material object which has been altered through human agency—there has had to be an act of imagining. Familiarity with the problem and a long period of unconscious approach to its solution usually precede the solution itself. Imagining involves sudden insight, as much in the most primitive discoveries as in the most advanced. That a stone could be thrown farther and faster than a man could run in a given time and so bring down game he could not catch, was of the same order of imagining as the discovery that the switching elements of a computer could be electronic. Both were technological advances having a large influence on the social behavior of the period.

All of the accounts of scientific method are detailed explanations of the testing of hypotheses by means of experiment, calculation, prediction and application. But what about the discovery of the hypothesis itself, without which no scientific method could operate? Since no inevitable deductive steps for discovering hypotheses are known, and since active, working empiricists are prejudiced in favor of the rational (not, that is to say, of all that belongs to reason but of what can be mathematically shown to belong), they shy away from dealing overtly with hypotheses at all. The solution to this problem, however, lies in induction, which is a logical term for the structure of imagining. At the present time no decision procedures exist for the discovery of hypotheses, but imagining how things are is certainly a way in which investigation begins.

Imagining works in philosophy is done chiefly through the process of system building. Every comprehensive philosophy is a system, and such systems are not constructed piecemeal but all at once as the result of an immediate insight. The philosopher has to imagine how he could build an abstract structure that would provide some place for everything that he knows. Plato for instance saw that a consistent structure larger than any other could be made by putting together the Parmenidean and Heraclitean views of the world. Kant organized the elements contained in previous systems by considering all of them as equal alternatives from the point of view of knowledge itself, and as contributing to the unity of the knower through his act of knowing.

METHOD

Less familiar is the part played by imagining in the life of the man of action. Such a man has ideals at which he aims, ideals, say, of wealth, of military control, or of political or personal power. Ideals do not remain vague but take more positive and concrete form. The practical man cannot plan actions having great reach in space or time without employing not only his knowledge of how things are but also his ideas of how they could be and how he would like to make them. He does not merely indulge in fancies, he needs them as a practical working tool.

There is a distinction between fancies and falsehoods which must be made at this point. Fancies are imaginings of what could be, falsehoods are assertions based on descriptions contrary to fact but referring to fact. A fancy is not a misrepresentation of fact, which is what a falsehood is, but an assertion of possible fact. Fancies may lead to preferred alterations of fact; falsehoods do not lead anywhere, they mislead.

The man of action, then, must accurately gauge the shape of the forces at work in his day. He must project an image of the present onto the future; he must try to guess both what is likely to happen, and, in terms of that estimate, what can be made to happen. Being able to project into the future those relations which are not actual in the present, is his talent. For example, administrative power includes being able to choose executives successfully, through the faculty of imagining what would happen if certain men were placed in positions of authority. The man of action immediately tries to put into practice what he has imagined, but he tries to imagine only what is feasible.

It is in the arts still that imagining is best known and most easily recognized. The artist puts together in a material object of his own construction certain relations and qualities he has experienced in ways which intensify those qualities in their effect upon the appreciator (which may include himself in another relation to the object upon later occasions). The object thus constructed is a symbolic object, and what is symbolized is what we should expect from what we know about imagining. For in order to represent the unity of the world the artist has endeavored to present a part of it as it should be rather than as it is. In the-world-as it-ought-to-be the complete set of internal relations would be much in evidence through a proper subset, and that is what the work of art shows. Thus the artist is a discoverer and producer rather than what, in the popular terminology, we tend now to call him—a creator.

Art as a product of imagining may be seen from another point of view. The image may be one of action. Consider for instance art as the symbolic expression of the contents of an attitude. Beliefs lead to attitudes, attitudes to actions, provided there is no obstacle. But when an attitude is held, and it is known that the corresponding action may not be feasible, often the result is what may be described as a sidewise emotive expression. This occurs in a work of art for those who are productive, and it occurs in the appreciator of art for those who are able to elicit only a feeling response.

Images are used in tragedy and comedy in ways which might here be illustrative of imagining.

Tragedy is the drama of the qualitative effects of continuous phenomena. What is imagined is how to produce a qualitative reaction to limited value just for its value and despite its limitations. The tragic artist must envisage particular situations which would affirm and feature those particular values of existence which have been singled out for an approach through feeling. The tragedian through imagining contrives to invent symbols which enable us to suffer the agony of what-is, because of what-ought-to-be.

Comedy is the drama of the qualitative effects of boundary conditions. What must be imagined is how to produce a qualitative reaction affirmative of ideal order by derogating the limited orders of actuality. In comedy particular situations affirm and feature the shortcomings of existence which have been singled out for aversion through feeling. The comedian through imagining contrives to invent symbols which enable us to enjoy the embarrassment of what-is, that it ought-not-to-be.

Both tragedy and comedy, then, operate by imagining, for it is necessary in both cases to suppose things to be other than they are, as they no doubt will be and always could be. What is remote or absent can always be reached through relations, and qualities are after all only the other side of relations, the affective correlates which impress through the feelings.

Thus imagining is not only a matter of image-making but also a matter of relation-discovering. For the appreciation of art, the act of imagining becomes one of recognizing that what has been discovered always existed for everyone as a set of possibilities. "He has shown me what I have always known but have never seen and certainly never felt before," is what the appreciator exclaims of the artist before the work of art. The appreciator of art is called on for a certain effort, involving a definite degree of imaginative projection. He must enter into the spirit of the thing, empathetically participate in the adventure of the comic or tragic hero; and, as the consumer of art, share in the feelings of the artist from every side except that of the discovery itself. Art appreciation is daydreaming in prescribed terms and under arranged conditions. It discloses how the appreciator would like to have things could he have imagined them as other than they were. Appreciation is confrontation; the appreciator is made to see how the relations he might have known can be turned into the values he would not have felt without the active assistance of the productive imagining of the artist.

In addition to the originative or productive artist (the so-called "creative" artist), there is also the interpretive artist. Imagining how a composition ought to sound is the work of the performing musician, imagining how a play ought to be produced on the stage is the work of the director and the actor. There is definitely a kind of imagining involved here, and it is authentic though certainly of a secondary order. It relies upon the previous and more important preparations of the originative and productive artist—the composer, say, or the playwright.

Art features the qualities of a structure, usually by means of symbolic represenation. A Gothic cathedral is a good example, for there the structure as well as the qualities are separately in evidence. Science features the structure of qualities together with their quantitative correlates, usually by means of equations. The mathematical law of gravitation for example gives the formula for the existence of certain forces of attraction peculiar to matter. The facts necessary to the artist are qualitative facts, qualities, values and the like. The facts necessary to the scientist are functional and structural facts, relations, systems and the like. Association, however, plays an equal role in both and its service is the same. For a scientist with a fertile but controlled ability to imagine, getting himself up-to-date with all of the facts and theories current in his science is like putting more pieces in the hopper. The proportion of what he can do with them is not a simple numerical proportion of what he has to work with, but there is a minimum amount inside which the imagination cannot safely be expected to function.

There can be little doubt that much of human culture is the result of chance discovery. But the activity of controlled imagining is chiefly responsible. It is generically the same whatever the field in which it operates, but it rises closer to the surface and becomes more visible in the insights of the working artist. In other enterprises, imagining is necessary; but it is not too much to say that it *is* the essence of the artistic method. Since the method is productive of qualities and, in its operation feeling is the leading edge, the artistic imagining appears there in its surest form and can be best detected.

TWO

Artistical Resemblances

The struggle for understanding is in the case of art made especially difficult by the fact that when we attempt to describe the lessons we have learned from the encounter with qualities we are constrained to do so in a language which was designed to deal directly only with relations. For works of art are particulars, and no less so because they are particulars which are symbolic as compared, for instance, with linguistic symbols many of which are general. In frequent instances of the use of language we try to assemble the relevant general sentences in order to show not the particular facts but the classes to which the particular facts under consideration belong.

There are reasons for thinking nevertheless that something can be accomplished by endeavoring to determine what it is that all of the arts have in common. Many *a priori* conceptions have been enlisted in the effort to isolate the meaning of art, but our preference here will be to approach the comprehension of art from the point of view of its achievements. We prefer to take the view from underneath, trying to look first at typical samples of well-established works of art and then endeavoring to find the properties which will make it possible to connect them. For this purpose we need to draw lines across works from diverse fine arts, neglecting for this purpose all psychological considerations, both those of the artist and those of that wider public which engages in the appreciation of art and for whom the work of art exists.

It will be my intention to argue that art is (I) substantive; (II) qualitative and relational; that (III) its method is the method of resemblances; and that (IV) it drives in the direction of ultimate unity, although expressed in the present.

I

Before it will be possible in this section to show that the values art refers to are substantive, it will be necessary to define both art and substance, for these are very old words and in the course of time they have been given many meanings. I do not think that this is necessarily a bad thing, for a profusion of overlaid meanings each of which has served some kind of communication only goes to show the breadth of concepts. Still we need to present them by means of a language involving some precision, a technique which can issue only from exact definitions.

I will begin with substance, leaving the definition of art to be given later in the section. By substance, I mean "the irrational ground of individual reaction." Substance never occurs merely as such but always in one or another of its two definite states. These states are the static and the dynamic. Substance in the static state is called "matter," substance in the dynamic state is called "energy." To say that art is substantive is to refer to the static state in some instances and to the dynamic state in others; for instance, a carving in stone is definitely an instance of shaped material, while a horn concerto conveyed through a pattern of sound waves would have to be called an instance of shaped energy.

Now let us return to aesthetic theory. Aesthetics is the name for a specific region of ontology, namely, that region defined by the qualities which emerge from the bonds between parts. A contrast with ethics will best make the substantive point. Ethics is the theory of that specific region of ontology which is defined by the qualities which emerge from the bonds between wholes. Qualities and relations are correlative. We can see this most clearly by comparing the subject matter of aesthetics with that of ethics. The good is the qualitative correlate of the property of completeness, the beautiful the qualitative correlate of the property of consistency. If beauty is the quality which emerges from the perfect relations of parts in the whole, then the One, which Plato placed at the apex of his hierarchy of being, is not the Good, as he supposed, but the Beautiful. Aesthetics becomes the substantive keystone of ontology. Things may be good for each other, but the sum of all things is beautiful.

It follows from this theory that the aesthetic and the ethical are world conditions, of which the human is an intense but very small subdivision. It happens to be that subdivision in which we as human beings are most personally concerned. Unfortunately, however, personal concern is no indication of position or warrant of importance.

And even if we ourselves are our chief interest it may still be true that the best method for understanding ourselves and our reactions may lie through an understanding of the whole of which we are parts and of how the parts are put together in such a whole. Then we will be better able to add to what we know in this way those special qualifications which are peculiar to the parts that we are. Thus the material universe from the standpoint we have established may be said to consist in the aesthetic and the ethical. It may be added parenthetically that it is impossible, evidently, to concentrate on both at the same time. Art and morality are in conflict, and it often happens that one can be pursued only at the cost of the other. Hence the familiar types of the "immoral artist" and the aesthetically barren social worker.

If the good and the beautiful are substantive, then an explanation is immediately called for; otherwise, how would it be possible to distinguish a dish of fruit on a table from a still life of the same scene? Obviously, all things with the exception of the smallest and the largest can be considered as either parts or wholes, but not all things in all of their contexts can fairly be regarded as either ethical or aesthetic. The difference is made up by the type of property selected for discrimination. The stuff of the world consists in values, and these run all the way from large outbursts of energy, such as the bright chromospheric eruptions called sun flares, to those slight traces of preferences accompanying the most casual thoughts. We are talking about the good and the beautiful when we confine our attention to qualitative considerations. Thus to say that the beautiful is substantive is not to insist that all aspects of substance are beautiful. And it is the aspect of the beautiful with which, as we shall shortly see, art is involved.

We shall be occupied here of course only with the aesthetic. And now it is clear that we must remind ourselves that we shall mean by "beauty" the quality of internal relations and by "art" the deliberate production of beauty in a material object. Art is the adroit use of shaped matter to refer qualitatively or symbolically to the totality of absent as well as present objects: the qualitative reference by one part to all the parts of the whole. What is present is never more than the very small sample of a class, and it is the absent objects by means of which the artist is able to elicit the most poignant effects. Thus Yeats:

When my arms wrap you round I press
My heart upon the loveliness
That has long faded from the world

It is possible to see how, despite the properties which make the aesthetic and the ethical correlatives, art diverges from morality in some kind of final way. If beauty is the quality of internal relations then art is that kind of material object which is the most highly integrated. There is a degree of perfection to reality, a kind of high polish, which does not indicate any need for alterations or improvement. The artist does not judge, he merely observes. But he does undertake something akin to the cosmic perspective; for if the universe be considered the largest of existing wholes, then all of its qualities are equally authentic. The artist does not fail to observe that the bad is bad, the immoral immoral, the evil evil. But neither does he try to change them or suggest changes, for this is not his task; there is nothing hortatory about his observations; he merely observes and records.

II

The relational nature of art is most apparent in its heavy reliance upon the discovery of resemblances. The familiar classifications employed in the standard studies of literary usage of various types of figures will make this point very well. Metaphors, in which comparisons are implied rather than stated; analogies, which make fuller comparisons; similes, which make exact comparisons; and even metonymies, in which there is a substitution for the name of something by the name of something else, and its subclass of synecdochies, in which the substitution is of the part to represent the whole—all are clear instances of the relations which are exhibited in art (not only in literature but in all art, the plastic arts included), in each case between diverse items whose similarities are qualitatively impressive only because their differences are so vivid. The comparisons which illustrate such resemblances are made by means of qualities. In such comparision the flow is always from the larger to the smaller, as though in an effort to compress great qualities in a small compass, but this is incidental. The telling effect is the resemblance.

I take it that qualities and relations are two sides of the same coin. This is seen most familiarly when quantities are correlated with qualities, as in the melting point of ice and the evaporation point of water recorded as degrees on the Fahrenheit or Centigrade scale. It might be best to think of a network of relations thickened or clothed with qualities. Except in art, where qualities are uppermost, we deal with qualities by means of relations, for it is these we are able to construct.

Relations as well as qualities are contained in the resemblances, and whether one or the other is brought out and featured depends upon the method employed. It so happens that relations alone may serve aesthetic purposes, although this is less often the case. The use of geometric configurations in art is a good illustration. In the plastic art of the Moslems, who are allowed no representation by their religion, there is the beauty of repeated symmetrical patterns. Complex fugal forms in music furnish another illustration. These are direct approaches, and by means of them a powerful quality is elicited, a quality that we have named the beautiful.

We are circling here very close to science, which also deals with relations, though in quite another way. Art, like science, is one way of probing into nature, and the results are, as we should expect, quite different from those obtained by science. For nature is everywhere dense and, it is likely, contains more than can be recovered by those two probes. There probably are many others, lying for the moment outside our knowledge.

We are concerned here of course exclusively with the varieties of the artistic method and these are many. Another and somewhat backhanded approach to relations may be made via the poems of Walt Whitman. Classification presupposes a principle of order, and the philosophies by which men have ordered their lives depend upon systems of classification, upon categories. But such systems have their limitations; and after they have ceased to liberate they begin to restrict. When they exclude more than they include, the artist must take account of this, too, and contest it. For every system does have a residue of restrictiveness. Some of Whitman's poems celebrate the break-up of the restrictive aspect of all philosophical systems *qua* restrictive systems. Hence the famous catalogues which Whitman put together; consider for example the "Song of Myself," Stanza 15, or "Children of Adam," Stanza 9, where he insisted vigorously on the phenomenon of abundance, and so shows how the profusion of completeness, which was violated by philosophical systems in the name of consistency, may be enabled to return with fresh claims and energy.

Given a sufficient number of relations, everything will be linked up, finally disclosing a whole of which everything is some part. The shuffling of the categories in order to substitute chance for order, just as with a pack of playing cards, breaks up the world in such a way that a more meaningful picture can be made by putting the pieces together again in a different fashion. The randomized juxtapositions which result from such shuffling shows how very general resemblance is in the world. Whitman reaffirmed the existence of the largest of wholes by implication, when through the fragmented categories he seemed to deny the legitimacy of lesser wholes.

III

The resemblances resorted to in art are not confined to metaphors, which are category free, but apply also to the contrasts and pairs of contraries referred to in the conventional type of classical metaphysical categories. Familiar examples are: the temporal and the eternal, the one and the many, the concrete and the abstract, the actual and the possible, the individual and the universal, the perfect and the imperfect. We will discuss these by way of illustration.

The best approach to the temporal and the eternal in art is through romantic and classic art respectively. The romantic seeks for the eternal values through their manifestation in the temporal order. The classic calls witness to the eternal values irrespective of the temporal order; it is a window on the eternal. The essence of the romantic is the pathos of distance, the self beyond the hills of home. The classic theme is the timeless: what-is as though it could-have-been, what could-have-been as though it ought-to-be. Nothing but confusion ever results from mixing the actual and the ideal, and all artistic effects are cancelled. Consider for instance those contemporary productions of Greek drama, performed as though they were Irish wakes.

The concrete and the abstract in art are much more complicated categories to unravel. The concrete is exhibited through the disclosure of the depth of qualities inherent in any material thing which has been chosen. Full concreteness is the aim of the contemporary artist, but he comes at it abstractly; whereas the abstract nature of the object, which was evident in Greek art, was reached concretely. The qualitative richness of nature is manifested both ways, but each is the product of a concentration on the other in the exhibition of art. All value, insofar as it is value, is permanent. Art provides ways in which the concrete can be permanent, usually by the contrast with the abstract: one factor at a time, in order to show the depth of involvement.

The contrast of similarities and differences between the actual and the possible is employed in art in works of the imagination which make a specific point of employing the impossible as though it were not only possible but actual.

Examples are not far to seek: Homer's *Odyssey*, Swift's *Gulliver's Travels*, Carroll's *Alice in Wonderland*. Conditions contrary to fact assumed to be ordinary require of the reader, as in fact they did of Alice, to "get well used to queer things happening." In this way, widening the world to include more than the actual adds to the connections and ties things together by means of resemblances that were not otherwise suspected of being possible.

The resemblances between the individual and the universal are perhaps the most familiar of all in aesthetics. For this is what is meant by symbolism in art. Symbols are signs whose leading edge is qualitative, and there is a sense in which every work of art is symbolic; that is to say, it is an individual functioning as a qualitative sign, and qualities as such are universal—as universal, certainly, as relations. Works of art are peculiar in that they are individuals whose qualities are featured in such a way as to make them representative. As individuals they point toward the universal, as symbols they stand primarily for the qualitative richness of nature.

Finally, the perfect and the imperfect. One familiar way in which the contrast is made in art is by the deliberate cultivation of the ugly. One thinks immediately of Baudelaire and Rodin, for instance. The transience of beauty occasions ugliness, and for the most part beauty is transient: chance encounters occasion more ugliness than beauty. But as every artist knows, an ugly part may contribute to the beauty of the whole, and in the artistic method such knowledge is often deliberately applied. Ugliness may be negative but its effects are not entirely negative, for in such a situation beauty inherently excludes the device of sublation. The principle of exhortation states: anything worth doing is worth doing well. But the principle of excellence reads otherwise: only what is worth doing well is worth doing.

IV

It is time now to connect some of the points we have been making in order to show the conclusion toward which they are aimed. It comes to this, that art is substantive evidence for the unity of being. By means of qualities, art treats everything in the world as though it were a set of internal relations. Art suggests the essential integrity of wholes. The need for beauty is the need for that kind of perfection which concerns the whole, the unity of all being in a single system, the craving of each part for the whole of which it is a part. Through the work of art it is possible to enjoy knowing that the world is a system. In this sense art is the religion of empiricism.

The more disparate the items referred to and connected by metaphors the more clearly is the unity made manifest. Metaphors and other figures are devices for disclosing the qualitative connections between remote substantives, and the more remote the more effective. For the delicate manipulations of sexual love Shakespeare in *Measure for Measure* (I, II) calls on a fishing technique,

groping for trout in a peculiar river;

and for a callous regard from *Timon of Athens* (IV, III):

O, a root; dear thanks!
Dry up thy marrows, vines and plough-torn leas,
Whereof ingrateful man, with liquorish draughts
And morsels unctuous, greases his pure mind,
That from it all consideration slips—

METHOD

It is necessary only to remember the figures in chapters 5 and 7 of the "Songs of Solomon,"

His legs are as pillars of marble, set upon sockets of fine gold,

or,

Thy belly is like an heap of wheat set about with lilies.

Thanks to the literary art, for instance, the contents of the world can be represented in a few words, and the processes in their combination. If elements so remote can be shown to be intimately connected, the artist seems to be saying, then it must be true that everything is connected in a familiar way and the universe is a unity, with the obvious conclusion that if this is so then everyone's place in the nature of things is assured. Art is the ultimate theology.

But it should be possible for us to render the lesson of artistical resemblances in a manner which is more concrete still than what thus far it has been possible to do. In order to show the inexhaustible interrelatedness of the method of resemblances let us look at the work of one contemporary sculptor and one painter.

The sculptor is Henry Moore. In his bronzes, and in particular in the massive and monumental figures of the 1960's, Moore has produced the art of the age of the hydrogen bomb. Like all great artists, he has his own method of approach by means of which he is able to conduct the spectator toward the very center of the power of being. After our epoch has been passed over, he seems to be saying, time and the ruins are all that will remain: the grinning skeleton in the helmet, the massive eroded human shapes in the park or on the plains. But these will be sufficient to testify to the colossal spirit of man; his efforts so much out of proportion to his size, his accomplishments so much less than he had intended, himself contained in the contradictions which he had created and which, in the end, are to bring about his destruction.

Art has its effect upon us at the most primitive levels within the somatic organism—not the forebrain but the more ancient structures, from the celiac ganglion to the brain stem and cerebellum. And the more primitive the structure, the deeper the effect and the more forceful its response. Emotional reactions are primitive: the human species has been feeling far longer than it has been thinking; approach-and-exploration is far more compelling a drive than the need to know.

The art of Henry Moore puts man back into nature. If men are to survive they must be like fieldstone, like stone as with stones in the field. The prophetic nature of Moore's art is that it may give us man after the holocaust of an atomic war, blasted through and left immobile. For his outdoor sculpture confirms human permanence. It cries aloud for the stillness of eternity and assumes that such a persistence can be carried out only in the most elemental of terms, which is to say, the most elementary—funerary relics from an aging cemetery.

The painter we have chosen to consider is Andrew Wyeth. His art represents a certain informal and unorganized super-realism, with its own characteristics: hypervividity, brightness, selection of obvious elements and relations, affirmation, seeming lack of interpretation. Wyeth's canvases let the selected elements speak for themselves without reference to their canon of selection, in a way the camera does not allow, and with a depth not found in photography. It is at first sight photographic realism, but Wyeth has proved that there is more in the direction of naturalism. Look again; everything has a value and is suffused with happiness and an optimism no film can bring out. Yet these properties were present all the time, awaiting discovery. For there is always a great deal in nature which is not apprehended in any of our limited schemes. The natural world is everywhere dense with qualities and relations, and our greatest artists are lucky if they can show us only a few of the more significant, for these alone are enough to be overpowering. In the impersonal world as it befriends man (for not all of nature is anti-human) there are elements which turn against him only in excess: sunlight, vast expanses marked for identification, and so a world which in its simplest and most primitive repetitions is guaranteed to last.

In the paintings of Wyeth the situation is not the one we might have expected from naturalism in art. There is representation surprisingly economical, surprisingly clean, with the rough edges of experience showing in a way which makes them, too, ready to be loved. Art can be as dull and tedious as life itself at times; otherwise how could it suffuse life with such heightened authenticity? Being "lifelike" does not always have to mean being exciting or violent; it can mean, more fundamentally perhaps, being concrete—a girl in a field almost outside of nature, almost lost yet belonging; a boy's torn collar; knots in a board; hay spilling out of a loft; sunlight on a fading window sill. The naturalism is treated by means of a kind of distortion which is required in order to give the effect of the penetration of the commonplace to a depth which is not ordinarily thought to be there; and if of the commonplace then of anything. That

44

sort of world and its features might have remained forever unknown had it not been for the insights of the artist.

The sculpture of Moore and the paintings of Wyeth make a happy contrast. Both have chosen aspects of human life with which to fashion a style in art. Moore's choice was man himself, man in his most dynamic phase, involved with a background for which he is responsible but which he cannot control, and which threatens to destroy him through his own machinations. Wyeth's choice is more static, and what his art seems to be saying is that man at his best is man against a background which he has altered the least, a background of quiet woods and weathered barns, and of people who seem to belong to those same ages during which an undisturbed nature has quietly endured. What Moore and Wyeth have selected are different things, and they have treated them by means of giant similes; man is like a rock or he is like a farm landscape. Other artists have preferred other types of comparison, and the more original the artist the more unique his expression; but all must choose metaphors of some kind if they are artists at all, for such is the method of the fine arts.

Art deals with what there is, with substantives. It deals with them by showing that each is related to the whole by consisting in all of the others, and it does so by means of qualities and operates by means of affects educed indirectly. Thus the trope is the essential tool of the artistic method, and comparisons of the greatest variety is what is required, of elements the more widely removed the better. The world, ourselves included, is connected by the ethical and organized by the aesthetic. The philosophy of value is one-half at least of the value of philosophy; the other half is logical.

Together they constitute all that we can know about ontology.

But there has been enough consideration ontologically of the substantive assumptions of art, and so in a scientific age the values have somehow got lost. Philosophy has been impoverished as a result, and its study abandoned in favor of the appreciation of art itself. But we cannot leave reason so far behind without paying for it in some way. It is not so much the value of art as the value of what art indicates, the overwhelming qualities which constitute the world, that have concerned us here. The road back to the missing elements lies through the philosophical consideration of artistical resemblances, toward which this study has undertaken to make a beginning.

V

Aesthetics in the educational process has been treated mainly from the historical point of view. This has its merits and it is not criticism to say that it needs to be supplemented. For comparative theories of aesthetics, which is what the history of art cumulatively viewed seems to amount to, suggest the existence in the background of some kind of structure. The discovery of just what this may be is a speculative field.

Presumably any specific proposal in the field could be criticized as the attempt to preempt it by means of a single example. No proposal is entirely innocent of this charge, yet a start should be made even though in the end the starting point must be abandoned; yet even if this happens it will have served its turn. The advantage of a new approach is that it challenges its critics to offer something better in offering something different, and in this way they acknowledge their indebtedness to it.

In this chapter, and especially as pinpointed in its concluding fourth section, I have sought to show what insights could be derived from a certain kind of understanding of aesthetic theory in general and of art in particular with respect to that wider world of qualities and relations of which the artistic is only a singular case. Art is disclosed to carry a greater significance when we are able to show its wider connections.

And as we have seen the disclosures do not stop there. For art properly viewed in an age of science emerges as the bearer of religious values and eventually as containing the elements susceptible of combination into a fundamental theory of philosophy. It could be the concern of a comprehensive liberal education to show how through the broader appreciation of art such connections could be made firm.

I have tried to illustrate these emphases as they appear in the work of two contemporary artists, one a sculptor, the other a painter. Thus, in addition to the pedagogic value of aesthetic theory, through the understanding of art there is the additional and much wider dimension from which it is possible to learn something about the nature of things. That art could in this way be systematically organized within the educational curriculum I have no doubt, for the outline is already there for an orderly progression from a simple to a complex presentation.

THREE

The Poem as Artifact

Human culture, it is beginning to be recognized, is a material achievement, consisting in the works of man and their effects, including their effects on man. It came into existence because man felt compelled to alter his immediate environment the better to reduce his needs, which are many and complex. If artifacts are defined as materials altered through human agency to serve human needs, then culture is a collection of artifacts worked more or less together. The more highly developed the culture the more man conducts his life within an immediate environment he has transformed into artifacts of various kinds each of which has a specifically assigned function in terms of the reduction of his needs. He has made over his environment; it in turn affects him.

48

If this is the case, then any department of culture would consist in a particular set of artifacts aimed at reducing a particular need. The area we are concerned with here is that of art and its theory: aesthetics. A work of art is an artifact, as I hope to show; and my illustrations will be taken from poetry.

In order to understand how the poem can be an artifact it will be necessary to revise somewhat our notion of matter, for everyone will readily agree that an artifact is a material thing but few have thought of poems in this way. The notion of matter to which we have all been accustomed assigns it a lowly place indeed, and all the things we value have been set apart from it. Art and religion, we have been educated to believe, are spiritual affairs and as such non-material.

Such an understanding, however, is predicated on an ancient and traditional but now very much outmoded conception of matter. From the earliest Greeks to the most recent Germans, from Thales, say, to Feuerbach, matter has been a common-sense kind of stuff, gross, inert, perceptible to the senses and resistant to change, hard, round, broken up into impenetrable bits, ultimately simple and solid. Clearly, then, spirit, which was conceived as not only apart from matter but also opposed to it, had to find another residence. So did the good, so did the beautiful and the holy. Artistic efforts, like religious ones, were anything but material. Artifacts, under these evaluations, belonged to the material sphere, not to the spiritual, and the two domains were held to be mutually exclusive.

Modern experimental science, and chiefly physics and astronomy, has changed all that. The discoveries which have come so rapidly in the last hundred years have brought with them a new conception of matter. We know now that it is complex, indefinitely divisible, rare and valuable.

Something of the complexity of matter is shown by the wide variety of atomic constituents studied by particle physics, at the present writing some forty different particles. Traditionally, matter has been understood to be always in one of three states: it is a solid, a liquid or a gas. Now we know that there is a fourth state; it can be a plasma, which is the ionic or excited state, and this constitutes some 98% of all matter in the universe.

The divisibility of matter is well known, beginning with macromolecules, then in smaller units molecules, atoms and atomic constituents. The further divisibility of matter is shown by the failure to exhaust the atomic constituents. Below the smallest particles, the electron, the proton and the neutron, there are now posited hidden variables which may represent a level of still smaller particles, themselves indefinitely divisible.

The evidence for the rarity of matter comes from both physics and astronomy. The distribution of matter is uniform, but with an overwhelming preponderance of volumes of empty space. Anyone who has seen the photographs of the earth taken by the Apollo astronauts from halfway to the moon and from the surface of the moon itself will have been impressed with its tremendous isolation. The earth floats alone in space millions of miles from the sun upon which it depends for energy and even farther from other suns which might have as satellites their own inhabited planets. We are alone with our little bit of matter and entirely dependent upon its properties and on such transformations as we can effect with it.

Matter itself may now be understood as bundles of frozen energy. It is bunched in galaxies and intergalactic clouds, but the bunches are separated by great expanses of empty space. If matter is extremely prevalent, it is also extremely scarce, a rare enough phenomenon.

Since we know of nothing that can be done without matter, it is immensely valuable. We have only to remember its highly volatile nature and its interconvertibility with energy in order to see it as an essential component of all activity. Spirit may be defined as the dominant inner quality of a material thing, and as such is provided by matter with its opportunities. Without it there would be none, for we know of no spirit apart from matter even though the distinction between them be preserved.

In terms of this new conception of matter, we shall need to be equipped with a new definition. Since matter will be defined only with the aid of the concept of substance, we shall have to begin by defining substance. If we define substance as the irrational ground of individual reaction, then matter becomes dynamic substance. Nothing in these terms is merely material; there is no such thing as a mere lump of matter. Matter occurs always in some form or other, and there are organizational levels of forms arranged in a natural hierarchy. What we call the physical is the first organizational level of the material, the chemical is the second level, the biological the third and the cultural the fourth. While perhaps it is true that nothing can be accomplished with matter alone, certainly nothing can be done without it. It is an essential component of all activity.

We began by wishing to show that a poem is an artifact. We have developed the theory that the new conception of matter makes matter essential and valuable. In its most developed form and at the fourth organizational level matter occurs also as artifacts. Now it will be necessary to show that the poem is an artifact at this level and therefore a valuable material object.

Let us begin somewhat further back, now, and try to provide some further definitions which will be useful in developing the position. Specifically, the definitions we will need are those of beauty, of art, and of poetry. Beauty is the quality which emerges from the bonding of parts in a whole. The tighter the bonds the greater the beauty, always allowing of course for the size of the parts and the whole.

Now it should be possible to define art. A work of art is the deliberate apprehension of beauty in an artifact. The work of art is an artifact like all others, yet there is a difference which sets it apart. It becomes an artifact by being a material object altered through human agency for human needs, but the peculiarity in this case refers to the effect on man of the artifacts he makes. If culture is defined as the works of man and their effects (including their effects on man), then the work of art is an artifact aimed at having a specific effect on man, not to accomplish something else in the way of reducing man's needs, as a plough or an airplane might, but directly itself in terms of its emotional impact.

The definition of art was made in material terms. But now we have the special problem of a literary work of art. How are we to treat examples of an art which employs language in a theory of artifacts? The solution is ready to hand. Language itself, in the sense of the great colloquial languages, is a material tool for which generations of social effort are responsible. It is as much a material tool as is a bulldozer, an airplane or an office building. It is a set of artifacts, as artifacts have already been defined, for it is composed of sound waves modified to carry signs or marks on a surface used in the same way. The signs may refer to discrete or continuous material things or they may refer to other signs. Or they may function as symbols in referring to qualities or values.

There is an arbitrary social agreement (often extending over thousands of years) that certain signs are to designate certain meanings. The uses of language are many: the storage of beliefs (in memories or in libraries), the communication of relations, facts, qualities, and all are accomplished by means of modulated sounds or of scratches on a surface. The unit of expression is of course the sentence which can be broken down into words. Both words and sentences are names; in longer form they are entitled to be called descriptions. What a literary work describes is a situation intended to evoke a feeling or an emotion.

Now the use of language is theoretically infinite. There is no logical limit to language, it could be extended indefinitely. A computer for instance could be set to randomize words in sentences employing the half million words in the English language in groups of up to a few dozen. However, in the literary art there are well-defined limits: the novel, the short story, the play, the poem. Sometimes the effect sought is cumulative; a novel is not intended to be read at a single sitting or caught up in a single impression. But other forms may be; certainly the lyric poem is. It is calculated to make a single impression unified very much in the way Poe once insisted. The poem in fact could be defined as that kind of literary work of art intended to have a single and immediate effect.

And just what is that impression? The language of literary art gains its effects through indirection, by connotation rather than by denotation. The poem according to the theory developed here is an artifact and as such it must reduce a particular human need. Poetry is that art which employs the established rhythms of language. It employs them of course to embody certain meanings which are intended to describe things and their values as they ought to be.[1] The poem works by analogy to arouse the emotions which produce pleasure in the hearer or the reader. Here the analysis usually ends, for it has rarely been suggested what that pleasure rests on. Mere pleasing sounds is hardly the answer, and mere pleasing ideas is not much of an advance in suggestiveness. But another alternative is possible, and it may be introduced here. Art serves to lend depth to the awareness of existence. The appreciation of art is not a mere passive experience but an act of intensification. We can see how this operates by examining the nature of the trope. The language of analogy is common in the literary art. The images of poetry bring together disparate things which otherwise would never have been mentioned together. And the more remote from each other before their connection in poetry the more effective the image.

Surprise at the vast connectedness of things is pleasurable because it is reassuring. It is reassuring because if all things are connected then there must exist a certain measure of interdependence, and if all things are interdependent then there is hope for us however lowly our station or small in the vast scheme of things. Since we too exist, then it follows that we are extensively connected. If all things are connected then even we may count in some permanent way and may have a permanent place in the universal cosmos. This hope was very much in the mind of the Jacobean poet, Henry Vaughan, when he said he

[1] See the discussion of the points raised by this definition in my *Aesthetics* (New York 1968, Humanities Press), pp. 256-259.

. . . felt through all this fleshly dress
Bright shoots of everlastingness.

My soul [he assured himself] there is a country
Far beyond the stars

and again, speaking of death,

What mysteries do lie beyond thy dust,
Could man outlook that mark!

The intent, certainly, is clear:

There is in God (some say)
A deep but dazzling darkness; as men here
Say it is late and dusky, because they
See not all clear;
O for that night! where I in him
Might live invisible and dim.

Unfortunately,

Man hath still either toys or care;
He hath no root, nor to one place is tied
But ever restless and irregular
About the earth doth run and ride,

and yet there is hope, because, as Vaughan tells us,

I saw Eternity the other night
Like a great ring of pure and endless light.

Poems carry the signs of the connectedness of all things both great and small, and with that interdependence a measure of assurance that we share in their permanent nature.

The images in poems are often emotional reminders by means of which the reader or hearer is made to feel the security which is involved in his connectedness. That super-identification with large and faraway objects which the individual craves as the price of his feeling of security and which is provided for him by religious symbols (usually themselves artifacts and often even art objects) is provided also and in a more ordinary connection by literary works of art which often take their images from common experience. Connectedness is as connectedness does, and no less because it is noted in the world of everyday life. The hedge poet, the Edmund Blunden or the Robert Frost, is as useful in this context as the more exalted and removed Milton or Spenser. It is possible to look for cosmic connections in lowly places. So Frost, for whom a boy swinging birches, a man mending a wall, the gathering of dead leaves, or just the sight and sound of a brook, is enough to carry the message:

We love the things we love for what they are,

he wrote in "Hyla Brook." His is a world of the largeness of the very small, of the significance of the apparently insignificant. He said for instance of the oven bird,

The bird would cease and be as other birds
But that he knows in singing not to sing.
The question that he frames in all but words
Is what to make of a diminished thing.

The small indeed:

The sturdy seedling with arched body comes
Shouldering its way and shedding the earth crumbs.

Similarly with Blunden, for whom a bee in March, a village green and a dried millpond evoke sentiments of identification. Blunden prefers the smallness of an English river to the greater majesty of sea or mountain. If you go to the river, he said, and behave passively, absorbing all the feelings its borders give off, you will learn of the river god,

That yours is the love to which he owns.

Blunden was aware that there are connections, and he called attention to them, as usual through lowly things, as in the poem, "The Scythe Struck by Lightning." It is not necessary to derive a moral or make a point of any kind, not didactically, at least; the small things carry their own significance if one but describes them. There is all the value in the world to be represented by the backdoor feeding of the poor man's pig,

Nuzzling the dog, making the pullets run,
And sulky as a child when her play's done.

But in general the more remote the more reassuring, and so in the end it is the grand conception which is the most gratifying, the loftiest image which is the most consolatory. It is the Homer or the Shakespeare who achieves the strongest effects in this direction, men who wrote about their own times perhaps but in ideal terms, and about events which for us at least are so remote that they no longer wear the pedestrian look. For Homer it was war, with the gods of Olympus ranged on the two sides and influencing the outcome, with sounds and cries that filled the earth and sky, and with victories and defeats that became earthshaking in their effects. For Shakespeare it was mankind, represented by every man, each a maze of opposites and contraries, each with his idiosyncracies and his humanity hard upon him, a melancholy love of existence, with despair overriding the gusto and with the infinite protruding from the finite at every turn.

METHOD

In Homer both men and events are greater than life size, as befits heroes and their lives. When Patroclus cried, he was described as "shedding hot tears, even as a fountain of dark water that down over the face of a beetling cliff poureth its dusky stream." [2] And when Sarpedon was killed by Patroclus in battle, "he fell as an oak falls, or a poplar or a tall pine, that among the mountains shipwrights fell with whetted axes to be a ship's timber." [3]

In Shakespeare they are bigger than lifesize, too, and easily as grandiloquent. Witness Cleopatra on the death of Antony:

> The crown o'th'earth doth melt. My lord!
> O, withered is the garland of the war,
> The soldier's pole is fall'n: young boys and girls
> Are level now with men: the odds is gone,
> And there is nothing left remarkable
> Beneath the visiting moon.

Witness Caesar's first words when he learns of the death of Antony:

> The breaking of so great a thing should make
> A greater crack: the round world
> Should have shook lions into civil streets,
> And citizens to their dens. The death of Antony
> Is not a single doom; in that name lay
> A moiety of the world.

Finally, witness Cleopatra's description of Antony after his death and shortly before hers:

[2] Iliad, XVI. 1-5. A.T. Murray trans.
[3] Iliad, XVI. 480-85. A.T. Murray trans.

58

His face was as the heavens, and therein stuck
A sun and moon, which kept their course and lighted
The little O, the earth.
His legs bestrid the ocean, his reared arm
Crested the world: his voice was propertied
As all the tuned spheres, and that to friends;
But when he meant to quail and shake the orb,
He was as rattling thunder. For his bounty,
There was no winter in't; an autumn 'twas
That grew the more by reaping; his delights
Were dolphin-like, they showed his back above
The element they lived in: in his livery
Walked crowns and crownets; realms and islands were
As plates dropped from his pocket.

Security with Homer was to be had from the grandeur of
the identification with gods and heroes and with at least the
nearness to cosmic events. Security with Shakespeare was to
come from the continuing nature of the human species and
the glory of its profusion of qualities, and from the knowledge that each and every one of us is no less human than all
others.

I have tried to show elsewhere that the skin is the organ
which carries the need of the organism for ultimate security
because it is the protective boundary layer and the outer
limits of the safety zone. The generic drive of aggression
involves "risking one's skin." Unexpected skin stimulations
report insecurity; and conversely expected ones, and particularly those of a pleasant nature, report security. If the
touch is painful, then insecurity, but not if it is pleasurably
cool or warm. It is through the imaginative effort that the
short-range self, the only self capable of touch, is converted

symbolically into the long-range self; and we can imagine—through poetry for instance—more remote contacts, contacts with large and faraway objects which have the reassuring property we seek, have it because being large they survive longer. The earth we know does; and the sun, and the visible stars, and the region beyond, all of which we suppose endure forever with an endurance which we wish with all our being to share with them. Largeness in space usually means remoteness in time. The individual threatened by extinction looks away from his small date and place to those "far off divine events," in which he would participate as though not being limited to a narrow strip of existence were natural enough for him. Poetry reclaims his own in this sense, and serves as a reminder that the limits of his daily activities are not the limits of his world, that he can matter more, from minute to minute and from place to place, than he seems to himself daily to matter.

For the poet takes us with him on his sensuous adventures. He leaves his poems with us as tools or as artifacts by means of which we are enabled to lift ourselves to the level of significance of value where everything that happens matters. He makes us feel in intimate terms the inner nature of little and seemingly unimportant things. He makes us smell and taste and hear and see. But above all he makes us touch; he brings our borders into contact, imaginatively, with the borders of larger and more important things, and by contagious magic restores us to an importance which we thought we had lost or had not remembered that we could share.

PART TWO

Practice

FOUR

A Behaviorist Theory of Art

I

In this chapter an attempt will be made to construct a theory of aesthetics by employing a theory of human behavior which has been extended from the theory of animal behavior as developed by Pavlov, Watson, Hull and Skinner. By "behavior" then will be meant here the movement of individuals so far as it has any structure, and by "need" what a material object can supply to an individual which is necessary for his or his species' survival. The theory supposes that all behavior is an attempt to reduce some one of a number of organic needs, and that such reduction is necessary to the individual's welfare.

Animal behavior can be accounted for by supposing that it is appetitive—behavior in accordance with needs. When a stimulus is introduced from the outside—usually some material object which appears to offer need-reduction—the animal makes responses intended to reduce the need, usually in two parts: a preparatory response leading to a consummatory response. The consummatory response offers the reward of need-reduction which reinforces the pattern of behavior.

Human behavior can be accounted for by assuming that the individual is an animal with added properties. The human additions are many, but I shall single out chiefly three.

1. The preparatory responses are more elaborate. A man does not lean over and lap up water when he sees it, as a dog does. He pours it into a container and then drinks from the container in accordance with the customs of his particular society, and all this usually after constructing reservoirs, purification plants and an elaborate system of underground conduits and indoor plumbing.

2. There is a feedback from the material objects which have been altered by the behavior. A horse tends to behave on every occasion just as it behaved in the past on a similar occasion. Not so man. With the use from childhood of chairs, he loses the use of muscles which enable him to sit with his heels flat on the ground, after the manner of East Indians.

3. Responses to stimuli may be considerably delayed. Behavior patterns of any elaborate nature are not usually retained for any length of time among the lower animals. But the human response to stimuli may occur many years after the stimuli. A young business man may learn of excellent commercial opportunities in another country, yet wait several years before exploring them.

All human behavior, then, like all animal behavior, can

be accounted for as a series of responses to stimuli. The responses are made in terms of needs, or of drives to reduce the needs. The chief needs are thirst, hunger, sex, curiosity, activity and survival. The human individual has developed the first three—the primary drives—in terms of the preparation for responses, and the second three—the secondary drives—in terms of education, science and religion. Thus while the human behavior is similar to that of the lower animals it is also far more complex and constructive. Both the complexity and the constructiveness can be seen in the transformations which human individuals effect in material objects. Let us call such material objects "artifacts" and define them as objects which have been altered through human agency. They are of two kinds: tools and signs. "Tools" are material objects employed to move other material objects. "Signs" are material objects employed to refer to other material objects. "Symbols" are signs with attached qualities.

There are lower animals which fashion material objects, such as the beaver and its dam or the bird and its nest. But with man the case is stronger. He has succeeded in surrounding himself so completely with altered material objects that it can be almost said that he has transformed his environment. One reason for the existence of such objects is that he has learned to anticipate his needs and provide for them. He stores water and food, marries, establishes scientific laboratories, builds cities and joins churches. Wherever he may look he will find himself surrounded by the material objects which he has changed so that they may help him to reduce his needs. That is in a sense what human culture, what civilization, is: a collection of such objects, the calculated sources of need-reductions.

PRACTICE

There is nothing degrading in the consideration of human individuals as animals with needs similar to those of other animals. While it is true that human individuals are not dogs conditioned to salivate to a bell by ringing it at the same time that they are given food powder, still they may be men conditioned to respond to the beauty of a landscape by being presented with a picture in which its most beautiful features have been intensified. It is certain that if works of art did not satisfy some human need they would not be made. Works of art are material objects in the world, they owe their existence to human agency, and they have their effects on need-reduction in the human individual.

The thigmotaxic response to the work of art is the sensitivity to confronted objects, in consideration of their perfection. The universe is large and its unity can best be apprehended through feeling. The appropriate feeling, as we shall presently see, is one of exaltation. The permanent objects in the world are both large and faraway. The individual needs them for their permanence which he wishes for himself, and so he reaches out for them in his longings, and experiences a drive toward them. But he cannot reach them and could not touch enough of them if he could. And so he falls back upon a substitute technique. The unity which is apprehended through feeling is beauty, and it can be symbolically represented in a nearby object which he can reach and touch: the work of art. Beauty is the reflection of faraway objects, which reduces them to unity whatever their size and distance. The need for art is the need to be included through feeling in the whole in which all things are parts. The need for faraway objects is what the work of art reduces. As an object the work of art is nearby and as such is a surrogate for objects which are not. It symbolizes for the individual within the reach of his feelings the immensity of existence which lies beyond his reach.

Thus art and the individual are connected in at least two ways. The first is the way in which the individual artist stimulated by something in his environment responds by making a work of art. The second way is the way in which the individual who is not an artist stimulated by something in the work of art responds with appreciation. The artist is primarily responsible for altering a material object in such a way that it is regarded thenceforth as a work of art. And the appreciator is stimulated by the work of art to make a certain response. We shall deal, then, first with the artist and the artistic process, secondly with the work of art itself as it leaves his hands, and thirdly with the art appreciator, reserving a few words for a last look at the entire involvement.

II

What is it in the environment that stimulates an artist? Obviously, it is not the whole environment but only some part of it. But which part? What are its characteristics?

Taxically what orients an artist to a particular material object is a quality it may suggest to him so that he sees how he could in another object exhibit a similar quality as the quality of the relations between its parts, that is to say, as the quality of its internal relations (beauty).

Perhaps art arose as a secondary development of physical technology. Men who made for themselves crude tools, such as chipped stone arrowheads and clay pots, may have seen the comparison between those well done and those better done. The delight in the difference may have exceeded the utility of either. Hence there may have arisen the notion of things excellent for their own sake, that is to say for the sake of the excellence rather than for the sake of the thing, and the product was the first work of art: superfluous beauty probably first produced and afterwards recognized as a by-product of craft excellence.

Scientific empiricism is new but empiricism is very old. The artists always were empiricists. Every discipline in fact has its own empiricism, which may here be defined as the derivation of abstractions from sense experience. Every abstraction has to justify itself by such experience. In science what is abstracted is naturally occurring relations and these can be represented in equations. In art what is abstracted is naturally occurring qualities and these can be represented only in other material objects in which they can be featured in a way in which they were not featured in the material object in which they were found, namely, as the bonds between the parts. Something in a face, say, or a landscape orients an artist in such a way as to compel him to react toward it. It releases in him a need for perfection. Somehow he sees in the form to which some accessible material object lends itself an element of perpetual novelty. He knows nothing exists like that—but it could. And if he succeeds it will. Aesthetic apprehension is a fusion of feeling, thought and action, all operating together in a single organic response centered on an image.

Imagination of this sort is a kind of analogical thinking. Strictly speaking it is neither inductive nor deductive, though it more nearly resembles the inductive variety. Analogical thinking needs both empathy and the facile ability to combine, separate and recombine very disparate elements, to which profound belief can serve only as an impediment. The releaser is the sensitivity to confronted objects, in consideration of their perfection, which is stronger in the artist than in others and precipitates him into action. The response to the stimulus of beauty is the work of art.

The activity of the artist is a species of human doing, an activity intended to transform some material object in the environment into a form in which the quality of internal relations is put forward as a symbol of the internal relations of the universe. Qualities in this context have a suddenness which is a result of the character of their presentation. It is by means of such featured qualities that naturally occurring relations can be bonded.

Art raises the question of the distinction between the artificial and the natural. The artificial is only the natural rearranged in order to concentrate certain of its properties —in the case of art, certain of its qualities. The natural contains all possible aspects, including beauty and ugliness. Art is more single-propertied; the artificial is either beautiful or ugly. And it requires the services of an artist to call attention in the artificial to the beauty of the natural. Every insight means that some subtle component of the external world has been apprehended. In this sense nothing is peculiarly subjective if it is true. But an artist depicts things in the condition in which we could wish everything was; so that if an artist builds better than he knows, it may still be because he knows and can express his knowledge best only by building. When mysticism does discharge into logical channels, as it does in the controlled imagination of the artist, there are powerful effects. Thus it stretches the individual's limited being out toward the wider being of the universe, through a common quality.

What the artist does is to ready through his consummatory response a preparatory response for others. The artists are life-givers. Without them existence would be empty and without significance, meaningless, a mere hollow round of habitual actions to satisfy primary needs. But the arts carry the secondary needs, they show the individual how to reduce our needs to know, to do and to be. They make nearby sources of need-reductions out of infinite yearnings, proximate rewards for needs which had extended too far in space and time beyond man's limited powers. To experience lawfulness—to know that something is right, to construct a symbol of such knowledge in a material object, and to feel some measure of surrogate survival—such is the need-reduction accomplished by the artist.

Making a work of art is "qualifying" an object, undertaking an extended qualification as a preparatory response, in view of operant learning. A technique must be known, a material object aggressively transformed, and a generalized being adequately represented. Qualitative research is a form of need-reduction for the artist as part of his need to survive, to put himself in touch with the long-range properties of existence, and in this way to associate or identify himself with the universe as a whole.

Art is the only true acceptance. That is why it may be a mistake to think of art too narrowly in connection with the beautiful. For the artist does not try to make more beautiful the beauty he encounters but he tries also to find beauty in the ugly, for it is the ugly which illustrates more graphically that beauty is the qualitative infinite in nature. Religion asks why, philosophy asks what, and science asks how. Only art does not ask; instead, it rejoices. It likes things as they are however they are, and strives to include them, the ugly as well as the beautiful, the evil as well as the good.

From the philosophical point of view art is the practice of

phenomenology. It involves the reading of meanings by means of the appearances. There are signs on the surfaces of material objects not ordinarily seen, signs of inner significance and of outer value. The inner significance is an essential quality susceptible of much condensation. The outer value comes from the suggested similarities of remote and otherwise dissimilar items. The qualities of far-flung relations indicate a unity of being by discovering the qualities of relations which had not even been thought to exist.

Such analogies are new discoveries—they require new languages. Unless an artist speaks a new language he is hardly worth listening to. If he employs in addition a new syntax, our joy at comprehending him at last will be in proportion to the difficulty we experienced at first. In this sense every artist strives towards an ideal language of his own devising, and many obstacles are encountered in getting from one ideal of this kind to another.

III

What is a work of art? The deliberate apprehension of beauty in a material object. We have already seen that beauty consists in the quality of the bond between the parts of a material object, but this needs elaborating somewhat. Beauty is the quality which emerges from the perfect relations of parts in a whole, it is the quality of internal relations. The artistic method consists in apprehending in a material object the quality of such relations. Beauty is in readily accessible form when the qualitative correlate of the relation of consistency in a material object dominates the appearances of that object. Where the quality of internal relations is featured in a material object (as it is in a work of art), it symbolizes a unity in which every separate part is represented as a necessary part of the whole.

A work of art, then, is a material object made for the quality of its internal relations. But let us consider such objects with respect to the representation involved. Another element then enters. A work of art is a material object in space and time and has to be understood against the background of other material objects in space and time which are not works of art. When the quality of internal relations is featured in a material object, as it is for instance in art, there is a symbolism involved of the unity of the universe in which everything—including, by the way, the appreciator of art—is represented as some necessary part of the whole. But such symbolism involves qualities in the present derived from possibilities which are only described.

That art has a formal quality can hardly be denied. We have grown so accustomed to the achievements of logic and mathematics that when we say formalization we seem to refer only to abstractions, but the question occurs whether there are not other kinds of formalization. To formalize could mean to render as precise as the material to be included would allow. Then we should have to admit that in art we are rendering something precise, but we should need another kind of precision to handle another kind of subject-matter, in this case values. To render values precise presents a problem of formalization in art. We shall have to find for it a different logic—provided we are to be allowed to use the word "logic" at all.

Thus we could speak of dream logic as the reason why scenes are juxtaposed in dreams in ways which are inconsistent with actual time and space relationships yet exhibit their own type of consistency. The consistencies of qualities have not been studied and dreams have been considered chiefly with respect to their psychological content. In a dream it is possible to walk out of one room and into another without difficulty, where in actual life the adjacent room may have been miles, and decades, away. But there was in the dream—and the dream will of course justify this on its own ground—some reason for joining these two rooms. They may for instance have figured in important episodes in a man's life which are quite closely connected despite many superficial differences.

A work of art, then, may be an example of dream logic come alive in a material object. In a work of art the artist tries to capture in a material the impact of an intuition. He never completely exhausts the intuition although he approximates it as nearly as possible in words, in clay, in the actions of characters, in the movement of human bodies, in sound or in architectural structures. Works of art are equivocal as the logic of dreams is equivocal. Only in this way is it possible to obtain the tensions which will invoke the proper values. In dream logic we cannot formalize without residue, but we can suggest the presence of what is omitted. The formalization of dream logic in a work of art makes of the formal work of art a system which includes in an important way what is excluded or omitted in other ways.

In art what is present is not merely present but represents the absent in the present. Just as a universal represents absent as well as present objects, so the work of art stands as the prerogative instance of a supreme quality, that member of a class which can represent so completely the other members as to be, qualitatively at least, identical with the class.

PRACTICE

The relation of a work of art to what it represents that is absent requires further analysis when we remember that the work of art also represents what is present. The distinction is similar to what objective idealists call the possible, and epistemological realists call the potential. Works of art can now be further defined in relation to their environment as "the qualities of negative constructions." By "negative constructions" I mean configurations of objects and events representing other material objects which do not exist and other events which do not happen. It was Proust who said that "The pleasure an artist gives us is to make us know an additional universe" (*Letters*, 228). Art is negative in the sense that it stands in exclusion from the positive contents of actual existence and in contrast with them. Art is the picture of possibilities.

Art exists in order to verify the authenticity of alternatives, through an endorsement of the genuineness and intensity of each of them by means of the use of a model. A statue, for instance, is a configuration in bronze of a man who does not exist as an organism. A novel is a configuration in language of human events which do not happen in any existing society. By the "qualities" of negative construction I mean the total effects of each of such objects or events considered as wholes. Works of art are negative constructions which are made, in fact, with a view to producing just such qualitative effects.

A work of art is a selection of possibilities which are not actualized except in symbolic form. The work of art is a surrogate of the representation. There is no such Wonderland as Alice inhabited, no such individual as Hamlet. In this sense they are both negative with respect to actual existence, and if they exist at all it is in the form of qualitative effects which, because they are symbols, are more powerful than the qualities of their actual and positive counterparts. Works of art are concrete only with respect to their qualities, and otherwise exist only as lower forms of matter, such as clay or stone or marks on paper. But as qualities they enjoy a persistence which would not be the privilege of their actual and positive counterparts. Hamlet has a different sort of existence from that of the live King of Denmark but one which lasts much longer.

IV

Works of art are material objects transformed through human agency, things made. But what is more, they are things made for a reason. The purpose of art is appreciation. The unconditioned response is the response to beauty, the "all-well" signal. The appreciation of art is a conditioned response, learning by means of the feelings something of the depth of the external world through the qualities peculiar to the objects disclosed to experience. The individual who is sensitive to natural beauty can be shifted to substitute works of art, with the result that the quality of his response is intensified. The art is useful because it is stronger and more concentrated. Works of art may be considered preparatory responses providing the permanent possibility of conditioning. Art appreciation is active self-conditioning. The man who has been conditioned by works of art will retain his intensity of appreciation when he returns to the contemplation of nature. In this way his aesthetic conditioning is an enrichment.

In animal psychology there are certain experiments in which electrodes are implanted in the brain of an animal and the animal given a switch, a foot pedal say, so that he can stimulate himself as he wishes, on the ground that he will do so if the resultant sensation is pleasant and not if it is not. In the work of art, conceived as what Mill called matter, "a permanent possibility of sensation," the human individual is "given the switch" when he is allowed access to the work of art, either through ownership or availability, concert hall or art gallery. The analogy should not of course be carried too far. The animal experiment belongs to physiology since it is not conducted with the intact animal, but the human individual confronted with an art object belongs to psychology because the individual *is* intact. I am not suggesting, either, that the values involved are the same. But the situation is similar in type. In both cases, an animal is allowed to stimulate himself if he wishes.

Works of art as artifacts constitute stimuli. We build them ourselves, it is true. But then they stimulate us. An artifact of this sort is a calculated and direct source of need-reduction. All artifacts serve need-reductions, but most of them do so indirectly. A stove does not reduce hunger but it cooks the food which does. But a work of art may reduce a need directly. It is not used to facilitate the servicing of the need by another material object but accomplishes this itself. Building a work of art is a preparatory response, but appreciating it is consummatory. The equipment of art plays an indirect and secondary role: studios, art galleries, theatres, symphony halls are parts of the preparatory response as much as the work of art itself is. But the work of art has a dual function to perform, for works of art—poems, paintings, concertos, novels—are preparatory responses providing permanent possibilities of need-reduction.

The moment a work of art is finished and takes its place as something existing separately, the activity of the artist is replaced by the passivity of the appreciator. For the appreciation of art is passive in relation to the activity of art. It exerts a force upon anyone entering its field of attraction who is equipped to take up the proper perspective. Appreciation, then, becomes an act of submission, a decision to be influenced or affected. The appreciator will feel what the work of art demands of him that he feel.

Responses to works of art consist in the more advanced sort of feelings which for want of a better word we call exaltations. Exaltation is the feeling of uplift. It is simple in that it consists of a single, uncomplicated feeling, entirely without parts, as any quality inevitably must be. But it exists at a higher level than simple sensations such as taste or smell. Implicit in the force of a feeling is a representation of the world. There is something external corresponding to the feeling, and no less so when the feeling is one of exaltation. What the work of art stimulates in the appreciator is the world-quality of exaltation suggesting it as a property of the world without change.

The appreciation of art, then, is a response to the stimulus provided by a work of art. What is to be obtained from the work of art is the quality of pleasure which comes from loving the world as it is. Not the passive "entertainment" of pseudo-art but an invitation to participate in the quality whereby things are related, which the artist has managed to elicit from the object. Art appreciation is an active enterprise, requiring effort on the part of the appreciator. Superficial feelings occur like waves on the surface of awareness, but deeper ones lie at deeper levels. They call for exertion in order to be reached. It is necessary to face in their direction with such capacities of attention as we have at our disposal.

PRACTICE

The necessary degree of formalization may occur as a result of the exigencies of rigorous communication whereby the artist informs his audience. There is a sense in which a work of art is the formula for a perspective. A formula of this sort tells us how to take up a new perspective on value, how to freshen up an old perspective, how to acquire a more penetrating perspective, or how to include more in our perspective.

Works of art suggest to the appreciator more than he is capable of experiencing without their aid. They point beyond the limits of experience, and bring "immortal longings" to man. Thus they remind him of his participation in being, which however small and temporary is none the less authentic, and offers as much of a hold on being as anything has. The purpose of art is not to give pleasure, though assuredly it may do that, but to intensify the senses and give depth to experience. Those who appreciate great art have learned to live more intensely. They have learned to know that there are in the world qualities corresponding to their most intense feelings.

Art is an effort to intensify feeling as another way of understanding the sources of being, self-conditioning by artifacts making possible a further penetration of the external world. Because of the artist we are able to see more deeply into the nature of things. Matter has at tremendous depths enormous complexities and powerful qualities; but they do not lie wholly on the surface. And if physics through the study of elementary particles can show us something of the complexity, art through the study of the conditions under which beauty arises can show us something of the quality. As consistency is to the mathematical system, so beauty is to the object of art. And as the consistency becomes more difficult the more complex the mathematical system, so beauty becomes larger the greater the ambition embodied in a work of art.

From the viewpoint of the appreciator the feelings quickly tire, and the more intense the more quickly. What stimulates is novelty. Thus the work of art must possess the property of perpetual novelty. The great work of art is capable of presenting to the appreciator a sort of permanent surprise. It is ever fresh, ever new. It is not common to find the world-quality disclosed in such an humble context phenomenally revealing itself as the similarity of diverse elements, and it is always unexpected, because feelings which resist resolution stubbornly remind us of their existence as feelings. A work of art is a stimulus in a given place that has its effects elsewhere, and appreciation reacts upon cognate experiences in the individual.

V

It is time now to step back and view the artistic process in the round.

The method of art consists in reacting to the quality of internal relations by building a material object with a view to featuring them, in order that the process of self-conditioning through exposure to them will be available to others. Such exposure is known to have certain affective and stimulating properties, through the intensification of the senses and the deepening of experience.

Thus in terms of entire man there is a feedback mechanism at work. What he makes, makes him. The stimulus-response system begins with an interaction but ends by spinning off a product. Nature and man interact to produce the work of art, and then the work of art assumes a permanent form. It takes over when there are no further changes in it, and henceforth continues the function of stimulating man in a certain way which we have endeavored to describe. The only protest which man can make to this now one-way process is through habituation. Too much stimulation from the same object evaporates the effect of the novelty and leads to an eventually negative stimulation. The cumulative effects of exposure too prolonged are deadening.

But then there are always new works of art. Studios are needed as well as art museums, and artists as well as curators. It is the new which keeps the old alive. The artist who is our contemporary is capable of reviving for us an interest in the classics of art by giving us a new perspective from which to view them. In art we are always standing still while the influences go rushing by. We withstand the impact of the past only to be carried off headlong into the future. We exist, however, at that point between past and future where the current is most intense, and we can feel in our bodies the tremendous passage of forces which lie beyond us, which are of a tremendous beauty, but which we can hope to feel only so much as our limited sensibilities permit.

FIVE

Concreteness in Painting: Abstract Expressionism and After

The argument of the following pages endeavors to suggest what might be the next development in painting after abstract art. Recently, nonobjective art has replaced representative art. In the latter, the object was present, whereas in the former it is absent. But traditional representative art did not fully represent; the object was held to be the same as its appearance, unity was sacrificed to obtain richness, and space was sacrificed to objects in space. The nonobjectivists discovered unity and the properties of space, but they overlooked the new knowledge of the object which the physical sciences might have placed at their disposal. In the next development in art, full concreteness may replace the extreme of abstractness of the nonobjective school. It will have to incorporate the resources of the old masters and the lessons learned by the nonobjectivists, in a new approach to the object divested of its mere appearance and laid open by the new knowledge which the physical sciences are in a position to contribute. Full concreteness has never been represented, and art for the first time is in possession of the equipment with which to approach this goal.

It happened first, probably, when Cézanne tried to endow the work of the impressionists with the technique and the profundity of the old masters. After that, the immediate future was decided; and the direction toward increasing abstraction established. Cézanne wished to add to the colors of the impressionists the strength of the traditional painters, and he wished to free the forms somewhat from their academic confinement. This called for a certain measure of abstraction. The work of such men as Feininger, Gris and Léger calls for a still further measure. Cubism was another step in the same direction, and the abstractions of Picasso were still another. The object began to fade; until, finally, it was destined to disappear altogether. From the abstractions, in which the object was represented in only the most dimly suggested sort of way, to the absence of the object altogether, was a very short step. And the nonobjective "school of New York," which liberated the painter from the need to represent the object at all, was the result. Nonobjective art, therefore, is only the logical inheritance of an extended development reaching forward from the impressionists.

What are the characteristics of nonobjective art?

First, unity. The whole canvas can be grasped as an immediate whole and needs no prolonged reading. There is in nonobjective painting an all-at-onceness which both makes itself available to the appreciator and overwhelms him with its effect, as though with implosive force.

Secondly, space. Nonobjective art studies the properties

of space as the paintings of previous artists had studied form. The classical painters were intent on solid objects *separated* by space but not *occupying* space. In nonobjective painting there is spatial occupancy. It is space as space, rather than space as adjunctive to objects, which chiefly concerns the nonobjective painter.

The two properties exist, of course, together, and the total effect is that nonobjective art strives to obtain unity by continuity in space and continuity by extensibility. Under the old dispensation, continuity was achieved by unity; under the new, unity is achieved by continuity. That is to say, instead of a continuity composed of infinite divisibility and infinite extension, we have the propagation of properties across space.

There can be no question of the tremendous impact of the large canvases produced by the abstract expressionists and the abstract impressionists alike. A crisis occurred in art for the same reason that crises always occur: the actual consequences of an established set of premises had become exhausted. To go on with the old masters would have meant to continue repeating in academic art the designs which had grown stale from repetition, a thing which they themselves had never allowed to happen. Nonobjective art undertook to supply the new premises. Bare of representative meaning and stripped to the minimum of content allowed by the requirements of the greatest degree of generality attainable through the simplest kind of particularity, nonobjective art succeeds in representing the last and most meaningful of all contentual statements, that of pure universality. In divesting itself of the object, the "school of New York" has divested itself also of what is individual, of what is dated, and of what is specific, and has replaced it with extreme generality, with statements holding only a faint trace of qualification and the least stain of embellishment possible in a formal language. The colored shapes on the nonobjective canvas are the formal symbols of an abstract system of communication and consist in signs invented for the purpose and limited to the reference they convey to themselves. The broad strokes of affirmation of Rothko, the small detailed weavings of insinuation of Pollock, and the rectangular assertions of decision of Mondriaan, are all variations on the semantics of self-reference. It comes to this, that abstract symbolism in art is qualitative self-reference.

Such effects, of course, were not achieved without some finality of revolt; there is a sacrifice of orthodoxy. A deliberate and orderly withdrawal from the sum total of resources available to the painter was demanded and supplied; for instance, the depiction in two dimensions instead of in three, and the abjuration of the use of that knowledge of perspective which had been commonplace since the fifteenth century—the century of Brunelleschi and Ucello. A kind of narrow scholasticism was adopted which sought to achieve depth by means of the renunciation of breadth. The arbitrary confinement to narrow limits meant that the huge suggestiveness of the concrete object was charged with divergence and interference and, hence, had to be excluded. The result was a permanent contribution: nonobjective painting. Freedom from the old academic restrictions, new conceptions of space and of unity, are not to be forgotten.

The value of art is to be found not in its effects but in its achievement. The role played by the appreciation of art is as extraneous as is the psychology of the artist to the object of art. Neither the audience nor the artist can ultimately be taken into consideration, which must center exclusively upon the work of art itself. Thus, to complain about the effects of the abstractive tradition from the impressionists to the nonobjectivists is to introduce a topic essentially irrelevant. It may, however, serve to illuminate something of the inadequacies of the tradition, and for that reason it is introduced.

The effects of art are felt throughout the society, to which the artist is responsible for supplying a certain measure of new insights into the visual world.

This world has hitherto been peopled with the ordinary objects of common sense: the objects available to a population engaged in hunting, fishing, agriculture, manufacture, and trade—in all of which pursuits there was direct contact. But the world of the average man has been radically altered. It has been altered chiefly by the technological applications of theoretical science, and the result is that the average man now lives in a world where he does not come into direct contact with the objects of common sense; he lives in the city and his contacts are mediated by a number of complex instruments which he understands hardly at all: the automobile, the airplane, the television set, the radio, the telephone, the atomic engine. He is treated not by herbs gathered in the garden but by drugs manufactured in chemical industries; he understood herbs, but he does not understand antibiotics. Where his understanding fails to follow the amazing complexities of his technological culture, advertising and the mass media of popular journals undertake to enlighten him.

The result is that the average man lives in a limbo of slogans and formulas, of pat explanations and clichés, all of which have been designed for him by experts especially employed for the purpose: the journalists of popular science, the public opinion consultants, the apologists for contemporary art. He never quite attains to the high abstractions of science and mathematics or philosophy, yet he has been robbed of his ordinary world, of the objects of common sense experience. He lives, therefore, an empty and meaningless life, suspended in spirit between an abstract world which he cannot understand and a concrete world from which he has been removed. He needs desperately to have concreteness restored to him, and in this need the painters could help. At the present he is fed by them not with the insights into the world of the common objects among which he continues to live, but with abstractions which lie well beyond his comprehension. What he requires of the artist, and does not receive, is a tremendous new concreteness—a concreteness which uses all of the resources of science and of every other enterprise in order to place man back in his own world with its objects widened and deepened. Nonobjective art, in other words, fails to furnish to the society which produced it exactly the values which that society so desperately lacks: full concreteness.

These contentions contribute to the main argument a serious interest in the next stage of artistic development. Will the immediate future supply what the present misses? In a certain sense, the "school of New York" marks the end of an artistic development rather than the beginning. It is a *reductio ad absurdum:* there is no way for it to go beyond where it has already gone. What further steps could be taken in the direction of abstraction beyond the elimination of the object? The end of that direction is the canvas in two colors and one form, or, more dramatically, the canvas in one color, or the blank canvas. These steps have been taken.

The program of nonobjective art stemmed from the deliberate effort of certain artists to isolate themselves from all the influences of their time, except one. They voluntarily gave up everything that had been learned about painting in the past, and they gave up, too, all the constructive possibilities which lay in the new developments outside of art in their own time. They accepted only the fashionable notion of abstraction as they understood it from the contemporary scientists. The result was a set of serious limitations and displacements along with the advantages.

The unity of the canvas, the all-at-onceness, was gained only at the cost of a certain over-simplification. When the nonobjective artist boasts that all of the values of his canvas can be encompassed in a single glance, he is admitting that there is not very much there. Gone are the multiplicity of levels of meaning, the profundity, the depths that require frequent repetitions of viewing. When a single glance suffices, no second glance is likely. There is the danger that, unwittingly, decoration has perhaps been substituted for art.

If the unity turns out to be an insufficient gain, much the same can be said of the new knowledge of space. The traditional painters had studied the space *between* objects, and the nonobjective painters studied the space *without* objects; but what about the space *within* objects? For objects, too, occupy space, and they do so in a way which distorts space and is peculiar to themselves. The space without objects derives from the space between objects, which is empty, and not from the space within objects, which is full. Thus, there are properties of space which result from spatial occupancy unknown to the nonobjective artist, who therefore does not study all of the properties of space but only those of unoccupied space.

Thus we see that despite the influence of depth psychology on some of the abstractionists, nonobjective art is not subjective. The subject dreams in pictorial images, including the images of geometry; and nothing appears to the subject that was not first in the world of appearances. Those who suppose that abstractions are subjective have not reckoned with the resistance of such abstractions to all efforts to make them other than they are. Nonobjective art has freed itself of objects, of representation, only to find that it has thereby accepted the limitations imposed on it by the nature of abstractions. These have their own set of conditions which must be met or deliberately avoided: symmetry, repetition, a certain simplicity which represents itself as complexity, and a requirement of variety that conceals the intricacy of design. And then, too, of course, there is in abstraction an object, one which is no less so for being a queer sort, and it is a segment of the pure quality of substance itself—substance defined as the irrational ground of individual reaction—and hence easily imposed upon by every sort of representation.

If art is the qualitative side of consistency, then abstract art might be described as the representation of the pure quality of consistency. The nonobjective design wishes to take its place, so to speak, as itself an object in the midst of the world of objects, thus adding to the number of discrete individuals; and the nonobjective painting is the effort to help it toward achieving this end. But this object, which is an approach to absolute chaos, is represented in the abstraction by a turning back to more primitive and less sophisticated conditions, to the formlessness of pure universal form which does not wish to commit itself to the form of any particular. From the ambition to depict only the objects of ordinary experience art has, as it were, freed itself and, in dedicating itself to the specific, has also become involved in more advanced types of symbolism in which the universal uses the particular by shaping it to its own ends.

The influences at work on the artist are not only those of art. The artist is to some extent a product of the art of the past and of the fashions of his artistic contemporaries. But other influences are also at work—influences coming to him from other disciplines in the society in which he lives and works. There is little question, for instance, that the most powerful institution in contemporary western civilization is science. Traditionally, the painter has endeavored to acquire any and all of the knowledge of his day that he thought might help in his painting. The artists of the renaissance were interested in science for what it might contribute to the solution of their artistic problems. Like Leonardo, they studied anatomy for its value to the painting of human posture and movement. They were not in revolt against science and in fear of it as a threat to art but, instead, relied upon it as an aid.

Yet, the nonobjective artist prides himself upon his ignorance of science and, if he thinks about it at all, it is only to hate and fear it, without encompassing the possibility that it might be turned into a powerful ally. If we look at nonobjective art not historically in terms of the painting that went before but in terms of the leading values of the culture in which it has developed, we note that it has been heavily influenced by physics and chemistry. Or, rather, the artist not familiar with physics and chemistry has, nevertheless, been heavily under their influence.

PRACTICE

The art of painting, like all other originative and productive enterprises involving intuitions, is not entirely a conscious process, and the effects of the physical sciences on the artists were not wholly conscious and deliberate; at the same time they can hardly fail to have been strong. The physical sciences are abstract; that is to say, they have started with the world of ordinary experience but have soon departed from it into a world in which the objects and events lie at deep analytical levels. The representation of abstractions in art has been in the same direction as the mathematical abstractions of the world of physics: away from concrete objects as these have been available to ordinary common sense. Thus, nonobjective art is not nonrepresentative art; it is, rather, art in which particular sets of abstractions have been represented. In short, nonobjective painting is not nonobjective at all: it simply has exchanged the familiar objects of common sense for the unfamiliar objects of the world of abstractions, as seen, for instance, through the electron microscope and the reflecting telescope.

Science knows what it is about, but the effects of science on art have to a certain degree been disastrous. The results are somewhat empty and poverty-stricken, being insufficiently filled with the richness of values. The effort to escape from nature into a world of abstractions neglects the nature of abstractions: the fact that they were *abstracted.* It is not possible, in other words, *not* to be a form in nature. The uniform effort to avoid form is itself a certain kind of form, because it is the result of a certain principle of uniformity. Pollock's paintings endeavor to attain to a kind of qualitative chaos, a state of perfect disorder. They could as well have represented a photomicrograph of cat cortex, or the paths of the molecules in a heated gas enclosed within a rectangular vessel. With a little patient searching among photographic plates of distant galaxies, one might find that the paintings of de Kooning and of Tobey are representational after all. The chaos of chance is as much a design as is any deliberate formal order; and to adopt a uniform principle of procedure, such as the elimination of the known visible object, is to achieve a uniform result which has its counterpart in some unknown but not invisible object.

Nonobjective painting simply rejects the forms encountered in ordinary experience in favor of those to be found in the kind of extraordinary experience that occurs in the scientific laboratory. It is a matter of complete indifference that neither we nor the artists have at our disposal the scientific objects corresponding to their representation in nonobjective art; for even in the case of the traditional old masters we rarely have a chance to compare the painting with the original object; we only recognize in the painting that there was an original object, on the principle that the painting was a representation of sorts. Philip IV of Spain is no longer around to allow us to compare his appearance with the painting of him by Velasquez. Since the heads of states of today neither dress nor groom in that fashion, we have only our faith in representation to tell us that Philip IV looked anything even remotely like that. Similarly, we do not recognize the object in nonobjective painting, because we accept the principle that the painting is not a representation of sorts.

Yet, perhaps this principle must be disallowed. How could one demonstrate that for a given painting there was no such thing as a corresponding object anywhere in the universe? What we lack is not the object but the representational *intention* of the painter. A nonobjective painting is a canvas painted by an artist who proceeded on the assumption that there was no representation because he himself was not deliberately representing an object. But since when do results match intentions? And if they do, then how is anyone to know? The work of art is to be distinguished sharply from the psychology of art, even though it is clear that, if there were no artist, there would be no art. We cannot sell a copy of the artist with every painting that he composes, and if we could, it might not be of very much help, because it is not settled that the artist himself knows and can explain exactly what it was that he sought to accomplish in a particular painting.

Despite the often confused aims of the nonobjective artists and the unhealthy effects of sudden critical and commercial success, nonobjective art has registered a powerful effect. We have only to appreciate it when it is at its best and, ignoring the dreadful work of the camp followers, wonder what is to happen next. No one with any intelligence would predict what will happen; but it may be possible to perceive something of what ought to happen. There is a sense in which whatever happens is what ought to have happened under the circumstances, else it would never have been able to happen. However, no harm is done by inspecting some of the elements that might contribute to the next step in painting.

It seems to be the time, then, to move in the direction of the representation of full concreteness.

Once more, the object must become the center of visual interest, only this time with two added features which, were it not for the intervention of nonobjective art, would never have been available; for full concreteness now means (1) that the space within objects is to be explored and not merely the space between objects, and also (2) that a new richness of objects is possible

1. Thanks to the study of space, the painters have learned a lot about how to depict it. Space is no longer adequately represented by the space between objects, for the nonobjectivists have not been concerned with that; they have been concerned with the properties of space itself—how it could be stretched, for instance. In the large canvases of the "school of New York," space is stretched to the uttermost and lies upon the canvas in an agony of revealment. Objects having this space within them as well as around them are now available. New geometries have brought new properties of space to light; but they have not yet been used by the artist. Then, too, sculptors like Lipchitz and Henry Moore have studied the interior of forms in a way which the painters could well adapt to their own medium, for they have, even more than the sculptors, techniques capable of disclosing the interiors of the forms of solid bodies.

2. The nonobjectivists have relied a lot upon the spatial properties of different colors, that some advance while others recede. Scientific studies, observations taken from chemistry and biology, could well suggest new dimensions in the interior of bodies, and a new richness of representation would result. The traditional painter had to be content to work with appearances and never sought to probe beneath them except in terms of such suggestions as he could discover on the surface. There were no other means at his disposal. Today the situation has altered considerably thanks to the researches of the physical sciences. New or-

gans in the human organism, new conceptions of organic cells, new structures at the molecular level, and enormous new constituents and forces at the atomic and nuclear levels, have demonstrated that the material object of whatever degree of organization is both porous and extremely complex. The porosity opens up the object to the view of the painter, and the complexity shows him the many dimensions now available for representation. Material objects as we know them are everywhere dense in a way that was not suspected before and therefore not taken into account by the great painters. It is possible to combine the old object with the new knowledge of space, to use color to depict intensity, to hollow out the object and to show its interior, its profusion.

In short, the abstract painters who were diverted by the scientists could now move in another direction in order to show the qualitative infinity of the concrete object rather than its abstract character. Science deals with abstractions, and the abstractive character of solid objects is a poor subject for the artist. But the qualitative infinity of nature is not a poor subject; to show it is his very aim and goal, and the end of all his efforts. The richness and diversity of the properties of solid objects have hardly been explored. When the painter was confined to the objects of common sense, he could still perform wonders; but what greater wonders have been opened up for him now that we know something of the complexity of the object and its many redoubtable facets!

If, as we have noted, the sculptors are pointing the way, then, in another sense, the architects, too, are somewhat ahead of the procession. The paintings of the current period resemble nothing so much as the architecture of the last period. Modern architecture, however, is in the process of getting away from its severe and unadorned surfaces, its unembellished planes and angles. Taking a suggestion from Moorish art, which was forbidden representation but which still found abundance of design in elaborate geometrical patterns, recent architecture has revived the grille and has embarked upon a new effort to intensify a surface by subdividing it, to procure continuity in this way rather than by extending it. Paint is intended to be brushed on canvases, and canvases are made to receive it. Every corner of a canvas ought to be hard at work.

The painters have now at their disposal a new approach to the representation of full concreteness. The dialectic of artistic progress moves from the representation provided by the art of the old masters, through the opposition embodied in nonobjective art, and on to the representation of full concreteness. Just as abstract art depends upon the academic art that went before, so the art of full concreteness must depend upon abstract art and revolt against it much as it had itself revolted earlier. The sterile nature of academic art compelled the search for a method of restoring that ancient power it had so degraded, and the abstractionists found that method. And then abstract art, in its turn, but in a much shorter time because it is a much smaller movement, ran afoul of its own shortcomings and so brought about the need for a substitute which would utilize the discoveries of both its predecessors, yet go beyond them. So in the same way that abstract art overcame and superseded academic art, the art of full concreteness should replace abstract art, and for similar reasons; for abstract art, too, has become academic and sterile in its turn. It is only necessary to look at the paintings done in the provincial art schools, and in the art departments of regional universities, to become convinced of the truth of this statement. It is time in the course of the development of American paintings for full concreteness, and the fully concrete work of art should combine the individuality of representation with the universality of abstraction in a unity made possible through the exploration of spatial occupancy.

By "full concreteness" is meant not the banality of representation of the old masters limited to appearances, nor the vacuous actuality represented by the abstractions of the nonobjectivists, but, rather, an art that would take advantage of all the techniques and skills of the old masters and the new lessons in unity and in spatial properties of the nonobjectivists. It would be an art that would take advantage, too, of the new knowledge put at everyone's disposal by the physical sciences of the abundance and richness of properties of material objects not hitherto known. Thus, the representation of the objects of our ordinary world would not be limited to the ordinary; or, put in another way, the objects of our ordinary world would be enriched with all of the properties they possess and which the artist alone can make it possible for us to appreciate. The qualities of the scientific abstractions do not give rise to abstract art—they have indeed never been treated in art— but they could give rise to an art so powerful that mankind would be gifted with a new insight into the unimaginable depths of the material world and a new abundance of life; and all this made possible by the greatness of the artist.

SIX

An Open Letter to Max Beerbohm

Dear Max:

Please forgive my impudence in addressing you. I am quite aware that we never met (although we could have: I was born in 1904 and you did not die until 1956) and that you are no longer in a position to answer me even if you wished to. You might be justified in feeling offended nonetheless, because my letter contains some objections to your work, against which you are now powerless to defend youself. I ease my conscience and perhaps at the same time lessen the offense with the knowledge that you will never receive this message. You are dead, while I am to some extent still alive, but I write to you anyway in the spirit that all men of good will are in some sense contemporaries.

I should add also on my own behalf that ordinarily I do not write to famous people or collect autographs. I have (I like to think) other ways of calling attention to myself. What prompts this letter, then, is my belief that I have something to say to you which might be of interest to others, and so I hope you will forgive some of the criticism contained in it.

Let me begin by saying that I was and am an admirer of your work. I find some of it too sentimental and some too superficial. Sentiment I take it is false emotion, emotion directed toward an inadequate object. Too superficial, because the object of the criticism which wit always contains is no longer around to bother people. The artist should always make sure that what he is talking about will not depart and leave him looking silly. That happened to the great playwright, Ibsen, whose plays are structurally second to none. Ever since penicillin has been found to be a remedy for syphilis there has been little point in agonizing over it. No *Ghosts* exist. And, again, no women live in doll's houses. More often than not there is a bitter note to your humor as there is to all humor which survives.

But I do not mean to suggest that all your work is of this sort. If I have a general criticism it is of the superficial nature of your targets. The careless lord is hardly the threat he once was, the world of the nurserymaid no longer exists, the belletrist is no longer a threat to the literary artist. Still, there was a quietness to your approach and a gentleness to its object which in these times of violence serves as a worthwhile reminder of how things could be and of what we have lost.

Some time ago you wrote an essay on laughter entitled, surprisingly enough, "Laughter" (titles are usually more misleading). Permit me to summarize the contents as briefly as I can.

An Open Letter to Max Beerbohm

You began by explaining that you could not understand Henri Bergson's essay on laughter, and you went on to elaborate that there was nothing special about it since you had tried earlier to read Schopenhauer with equal lack of success. An attempt to understand William James on Pragmatism was your last effort in that direction and it fared no better.

You saw of course the danger of the anti-philosophical position, that it involved you inadvertently in the holding of a philosophy of sorts. You said so; but then you changed the subject, as though the recognition and the announcement of a serious difficulty robbed it of its force. I do not think that it does and I think you would have shrunk from accepting its implications had you possessed the inclination to explore the position into which your thinking had led you. To see a danger, to admit its threat and then not to seek to avoid it may be fatal. Max, I insist you did not avoid it and so were crippled by it.

A quick evaluation of the meaning of such failure led you to a simple dilemma. Either these thinkers were not profound or you were a fool. You also, gratuitously, as it seems to me, slipped in a negative evaluation in passing when you remarked on your "failure to keep pace with the leaders of thought as they pass into oblivion." I am not aware that this assumption was anything more than a prophesy which was doomed to the fate usually accorded to prophesies. Time—by which we mean not the mere passage of events but also and chiefly the repetition of instances accompanied by some improvement in perspective—does reverse many values, and it is difficult to tell who has won a race until it is over, and so prophesies, which are readings taken from a contemporary position, are usually wrong. This one was wrong for Bergson is still with us because some of his observations have proved to be correct and begin to appear to have permanent value. Bergson's philosophy has taken its place among the enduring things, while Beerbohm's satire and the objects of it have both been swept away.

You did not find Bergson's book on laughter funny. I should not think you would, or that anyone would. Indeed it was not meant to be. Theories of laughter are no laughing matter; they are serious. But it just happens that they serve a purpose in heightening the effect of comedy. Understanding a thing is no hindrance to its enjoyment, though both understanding and enjoyment may have to take an assigned order in time. Theories of counterpoint and harmony do not make beautiful sounds, they may not make any sounds at all; but their understanding does lead to the intensification of the effects of beautiful sounds. There is nothing dramatic in the study of play structure but it may lead to the construction of great drama.

There is of course always the possibility that I do not understand you and that thereby I do you an injustice, but you have taken care of that. For you reinforced your position by shifting the argument from an attack on the abstract analysis of laughter to the presentation of a number of true comedies which have produced genuine laughter. Indeed you could not go wrong: they always do, you played it safe—Moore's *Life of Byron*, Boswell's Dr. Johnson, Shakespeare's Falstaff and finally a personal friend of yours whom you conceal behind the eponym, "Comus."

I said you could not go wrong—I meant of course the middle two. Your example of what amused Byron is not now calculated to set us off into paroxysms of laughter. As for "Comus," we have no examples, only your word, which

I would be inclined to take in any context but this. You certainly have demonstrated many times that you know how to produce laughter, indeed that was your professional career, and you did it well. But I cannot allow you to add "Comus" to the other names you mentioned when you provided us with no examples of his laughter-producing qualities, you told us of nothing funny that he said or did, only gave us your assurance that by not knowing him we were missing something.

It is not important, but I do get your main points. Bergson's essay on laughter is abstract. Dr. Johnson's and Falstaff's remarks are concrete. Laughter is concrete. Therefore true laughter belongs to Johnson and Falstaff and not to Bergson. Philosophers are spoilsports who take the joy out of life. How much better it is to live. Theories of laughter are composed by spoilsports, laughter is produced by living and palpitating human beings who offer life in the round, not a dry and dull version of it.

I wish only that I knew where to begin to set you straight. Well, let us begin here. First of all, it is not necessary to choose. There is a time for both; a time for theories and a time for practice, a time for thought and a time for emotions, a time to study and a time to enjoy.

Secondly, the two are not as divorced as I have made them seem. Understanding *increases* enjoyment. It does not detract from an activity to have shown it in depth. The measure of the strength and the profundity of a culture is the extent to which it is able to produce and support philosophers. Their very existence offers clear evidence of the presence of philosophy in the culture which they are merely reflecting.

Calling names never accomplished anything, and there

is no more ugly name to call an Englishman than to say that he sounds more American than European. But that is the situation. Since when was lack of understanding counted a virtue in European literary and intellectual circles? It is more of an American virtue. For despite the existence of American philosophers, men like Peirce and James and Dewey, it is the boast of almost all Americans these days that they neither understand nor read philosophy. Few Americans read philosophy, and the writers are no exception. We have novelists in the United States, and powerful ones, but surely none whose work can bear comparison with the greatest Europeans of the same period, none who can stand up to Proust, Joyce and Gorky. In heaping scorn on philosophy, and in another country, you have been right up with your day, but I wonder whether that is the kind of distinction you sought? Philosophy has always been an integral part of the literary life in every age when literature achieved greatness. Aristophanes made fun of Plato's theory of forms in his play *The Clouds* but he could not have done so had he not read and understood it. And by writing his satire did he not pay tribute to its importance in Greek culture? I am not aware that he left any legacy of disavowal, any boast that he could not read Plato.

In Europe writers have long sought out and read the greatest thinkers. Dostoyevsky sent for his copy of Hegel from Siberia, but I am not mindful that he was merely a Hegelian. Proust learned a lot no doubt from his two favorite philosophers, Leibniz and Bergson, yet his work is no mere echo of theirs. If Americans produce scores of excellent comedians it is because they live at the superficial level where comedy alone will serve as a revaluation of the values. This is a virtue, but at the same time it is not enough.

A culture with any depth turns up tragedies as well. But there are no great American tragedies. O'Neill alone wrote tragedies but in the words of Browning his reach exceeded his grasp. Give him credit, for he tried though he failed. Perhaps his failure only means that he suffered from the limitations of all Americans, the failure to reach down to philosophy in the culture, the failure to put down roots and to reach depths where wider meanings serve as a reinforcing underpinning.

It happens that we did have an important philosopher in the United States, though I doubt that the literary world even knows his name. It is significant perhaps that he confessed to a blind spot regarding art. He did not understand what art is about, he admitted, and so he did not develop an aesthetic theory as all full-scale philosphers do. Yet he was an American philosopher of size. He was one of your contemporaries and he was first recognized in England, but I cannot fault you for not knowing about him. I would have been content if you had read your own.

The faint gleams of false values lurk behind some of your essay on laughter, such as the poking of fun at the men who have wanted to understand comedy. I read, and as I read I lift my head and recall some other of your writings which are funny at first reading but will not stand a second thought. I was not unfortunately a member of your circle, but I wonder, I just wonder, whether anyone in it fared too well. You wrote another essay entitled "Hosts and Guests" in which you divide people irrevocably on the basis of the assumption that they are from birth either the one or the other. A good point surely, and who among us has not met specimens of both kinds? Well and good, until you felt called upon yourself to stand up and be counted. And then you lined up with the native guests. Guest—the more polite term is "diner-out." No doubt you were a great one, like your own Watts-Dunton or Browning, as you say. There were others who paid their way with wit and entertainment, like Sydney Smith.

That gave me pause, I confess. I am beginning to suspect that comedy is not the simple affair I once thought it, and that there are complex strains interwoven with it that I know little about. For your disinclination to entertain people who have graciously entertained you can hardly be counted a virtue. If it is funny, then it misses me. In my world nothing so rude can be funny. I know of a famous comedian who is alive today and who practices what you preach. He does not attempt to make a virtue of it, so far as I know he may not even acknowledge it; but I know some of his friends who hosted him many times without ever having been wined and dined in their turn. That is support for your thesis, but I do question whether it is the kind of support you anticipated or would even want.

Your admirers will condemn me if they ever read this, for they will say that I have brought up the heavy guns to attack a man who never made a heavy claim, who devoted himself to the perfect line and the ironic understatement, and who was without doubt one of the funniest men of his day. I admit all this and I place myself among his most enthusiastic admirers. I have only addressed this letter to you because on one occasion I caught you out, and it was only one but one may have been enough to show the seamy underside of a comedian whose objects of laughter are in danger of dying with him and of dragging his books down with them. There was a time surely when English decorum stood solidly behind the conquests of Empire, when all

English youth of the upper classes—a small but crucial number, since they did grow up to lead the others and to lead them very well—were not only raised by nursemaids but were saturated from the start with the nursemaid's view of the world. But that time has passed, and we scent a whiff of its gentleness and wisdom and folly in what you make fun of. But alas future generations will not bother. Only comedies more robust or comedies aimed at perennial foibles are likely to survive.

Aristotle remarked that tragedies are about those who are better than ourselves while comedies are about those who are worse. The description does not fit your work, for you have made fun of the upper classes exclusively. The reason may not be a good one, nevertheless that is what you did. You made fun of extravagant lords and of poets who could not cope but who, thanks to someone's income, their own or another's, did not have to. You made fun, in a word, not of the powerful men of the upper classes, but the weak ones and, in terms of personal living at least, the failures.

The members of the lower classes, you frankly admitted, you did not like. You had, as you yourself said in an essay on "The Humor of the Public," "no love for the public." Your concern, and I suspect your sneaking admiration, was for the world of the dandies, of rich, self-indulgent aristocrats, of precious *litterateurs*. Galsworthy was writing about the middle class, Dickens and D.H. Lawrence about the lower classes. But they were both writing about people, you were writing only about fancies and foibles. Even the writers you wrote about did not fare too well; witness "Enoch Soames" and Swinburne. You were occupied, in short, if I may sum it up, with the trace elements of the manners of one of those rare quiet periods in the life of the central city which was safe on an island in a day of Empire.

Not that I would carry my argument to its conclusion in a total denial. Far from it. Your work exists indubitably and has it place in the scheme of letters. I might want to insist that it is a small place, and I might even claim that with the passage of centuries it has no permanent place at all. And I might compare it to those delicate traceries of clouds on a fair day which exist momentarily and are seen and admired but do not even pretend to take their place along with the understanding of the regularities which are to be discerned in the larger movements of vapor trails and wind currents and the passing condensations of moisture.

There is a certain charm and a poignant wistfulness in contemplating the issues in which your sense of humor involved you even so. We see it from the perspective of a day when our writers are preoccupied with violence, with aggression, and with sex as a form of aggression; and when our young people see civil disorders of a warlike magnitude as the only answer to a war that they do not want; they think it nothing to injure people and destroy property because they do so, they say, in the interests of peace. Against the contemporary background of such disintegration and danger it is a pleasure to be reminded of how peaceful life can be as we look through the window which you have furnished us on the small errors of our ways.

SEVEN

The Art of the Philosophy of Art

The philosophy of art does not tell anyone how to be an artist. Nor even how to be an appreciator. It does attempt to describe something of the relations with them which every work of art has. For as it happens the philosophy of art is an art, not a science; and not one of the fine arts, either, but only a technique for estimating what is retained, what is assumed, what is implied, what is ahead, in the way of methodological considerations.

Philosophy itself in this connection is a kind of enriching examination, based on strict principles. The philosophers do not agree about the choice of principles but they do agree about the rigor with which deductions are made from them and they always aim to produce by their means a system of ideas more general and inclusive than any other. That, everyone will have to admit, is a curious situation to say the least: logical precision placed in operation upon the results of imaginative guessing. These days the possession of large amounts of information is quite common, though few are able to meet the demand for organization such knowledge entails. And so for the most part it lacks unity.

Those who do hold their knowledge under the conditions imposed by the need for consistency find that they have a philosophy. And of course there are advantages to be gained in this way. To move against a background of principles, however unstated they be, means to look deeper into the nature of things and hence to live more intensely. We can only take in, only absorb, what we find out about, a fact which makes of our inner intensity a function of outer principles.

The tenacity of belief is encountered before its content. All the same it comes as something of a shock that the quantity of knowledge which is held as belief is a constant. Everyone has the same amount of knowledge if knowledge be defined as the sum of beliefs about the outer world and the inner world. There is no such thing as ignorance when ignorance is understood as the absence of knowledge. It would be better to define it as the possession of false knowledge. Henry Ford once said that history is bunk. That was his theory of history, and it was all-inclusive if nothing else. Other men go more into the details and not all agree with his implied conclusion, but some do share with him the possession of a comprehensive theory of history.

The thing about philosophy is that you can ignore it but it won't ignore you. If you ignore it, the same statement can be made: that if your beliefs are consistent you assume the principles which underlie the beliefs. And since beliefs do lead to actions, then if your beliefs are inconsistent your actions will be self-defeating for you will do things which have conflicting effects.

Philosophy as a starting point is a matter of getting back to very small beginnings, to a presuppositionless first move. The ideal of course would be to start with nothing at all, a thoroughgoing standpointlessness. But that is only possible for a metaphysics, not for any undertaking with a less fundamental involvement. There is a starting point if there are definitions, for definitions lead to axioms and what follows from them tends to be theorematic in character. Here in the philosophy of art where we lack the proper metaphysical approach we can do no less. Accordingly, our starting point will consist in two definitions, one of beauty (to prepare the ground), and one of art.

Let us see first, then, if we cannot say what beauty is. It is the quality which emerges when in a material body there is a harmony of parts. Another way to put this would be to say that beauty is the high quality of internal relations (these are said to be high when the relations are perfect or near perfect).

And now for art. A work of art may be defined as a material body which has been altered deliberately in order to feature its beauty. The term, material body, has to be understood to include not only bronze or stone and paint on canvas but also printed words and sound waves, anything in fact which can serve as an art medium.

You see that I have defined art without reference to the senses, and indeed without reference to the artist. I have merely said what art is, and it would follow that those who produce art are artists. I did it this way because I wanted to be able to show that the philosophy of art rests on the work of art and not on the psychology of the artist. No one would deny the importance of the artist in the production of art: obviously, without the artist, in most instances there would be no art. (In some instances we would have the spectacle of aesthetic objects, such as a sunset or a particularly beautiful piece of driftwood, the value of which may lie very close to those works of art which were made by man.) But the accidental works of non-human nature however high their value are still not art. Deliberation allows for a greater complexity and hence for a greater intensity in a small compass.

To the sculptor when he has completed the modelling of a statue it becomes a thing out in the world capable of standing on the merits of its own contained values. And until it becomes possible to sell a copy of the sculptor with every cast of the sculpture, this must remain true. But the sculptor dies and the statue does not; it is still to be found in the gallery for all to see and appreciate, and no row of words could make its meaning any clearer.

That is why I have chosen to approach the whole topic of the philosophy of art through the work of art itself. For a guide to its meaning the work of art must remain the only primary source. I agree of course that it has external relations, and that many of these come to it through the artist. But one can look behind him for their origins and find them in the culture. The arts have many things in common with other enterprises in the same culture as well as points of similarity with the arts of other cultures. The arts influence and are influenced by other institutions. Cultural conditioning, although evasive and transparent, affects everything.

The artist is always free to do whatever he wishes to do, but it happens that what he wishes to do bears a striking similarity to other movements in the same culture. For he is limited to his own knowledge and experience, and his imagination is confined to them. He does not feel the constraint this imposes but instead he feels free within the culture because he rarely encounters its boundaries. What he needs in order to operate as an artist is sufficient mental chaos to allow for the elaborate random flow of ideas and impressions past each other. His controlled imagination is on the watch for far-flung resemblances, which are brought to the surface in this way. The contiguity of images makes possible the detection of significant similarities and contrasts.

In the Middle Ages when no pioneering was called for and everyone knew his alloted task, the artists were artisans who made their own art materials and dissected their models. By contrast the later method of buying materials and copying appearances, though advertised as naturalistic is not so. It results in a kind of abstraction.

The Italian Renaissance saw the combination of the sensuous and the intellectual which had been so well balanced by the Greeks. Those artists who managed the rebirth of Greek art in the new setting provided by the Italian city-states sought to combine an individualism of expression with a panorama of existing beliefs, chiefly taken from the Roman Catholic version of Christianity. And a magnificent equilibrium was achieved if only for a second by the passions which were straining to transmute violence into a static representation without the loss of spiritual power.

Now in our own time with the banishment of representation the intellectual and the abstract predominate in art. Space has replaced the object in space, but the balance has been lost. In our own day the plastic arts have been influenced by the rise of the science of physics, which investigates nature by means of abstract hypotheses and planned experiments. The hypotheses are mathematical and the method instrumental, and so they have become somewhat more removed than art can manage. Consider for instance the action art in which the painter uses his own body as a brush or his model when he rolls her around on the canvas. One senses a limiting case in this direction and a dead end. There isn't very much to be seen down that way. Art may die from trying too hard, though this is possible only for a while, for perhaps a generation, say. For there are timeless elements in both science and art, even though the selection is quite different: qualities for art and relations for science.

It might be helpful if we were to use an example, otherwise mentioning qualities and relations might not mean anything specific. Therefore let us compare the way space is treated in contemporary physics with the way it is treated in modern art—in sculpture, to be more specific.

Space in modern physics is the locus of the possibility of material bodies, a system of properties borrowed from objects in space. It is the world which such bodies have in common, such as symmetry, reversibility and graininess, and it could not exist apart from them. From the here-now of any body, there-now is the locus of some other body. Bodies alter one another in space, which is thus the region of relative affectability.

Space in contemporary sculpture is the object with which the sculptor is primarily concerned. He endeavors to get at the internal features of the shapes on which he is working. Such shapes are malleable and isolable, making it possible to replace representative forms by abstractions. Space itself can be manipulated in the absence of representation by those properties of space itself which are present in material bodies.

And so now the cry is: back to the object, but treated how? That depends henceforth upon the direction taken by the culture. Artists have reliable aims because in their own persons they are the sensitive recording mechanisms which receive impressions too subtle to be felt by others. Cultural influences in this way may be both powerful and predictive. The artists are the true prophets, they feel the atmosphere of what is going to happen before it does. They cannot say so directly but they can express it by means of feeling.

Judging by the art of the day, by the canvases of de Kooning and Johns, for instance, or the music of Stockhausen and Cage, the outlook for the culture is not good. The break up of the forms suggests the destruction of all feeling, and the turn of art in the direction of abstraction presages the disintegration of the social order. But there are some signs of hope. In many a contemporary painting we see the representation peeping out from behind the abstraction, as though it were saying, "May I come out now?" Watch at the corners of the Rothko-like panel for the emergence of a semiclassical figure.

Art has other features beside prophecy, of course. It may also be considered apart from its connections with the culture, as though it were an autonomous element in the world, in which case its values are intrinsic or extrinsic (or both).

Intrinsically, the work of art is a concretely particularized system of ontology, seen qualitatively as an organization of bonds between parts. It is a consistent system with elements which correspond to facts in the actual world. Thus the work of art is not merely something well made but something made to be well made, and for no other end.

Extrinsically, art furnishes a form of vicarious aggression, capable of drawing off in a harmless way drives which might otherwise have been destructive. In this connection it may be compared with sport. Both have to do with aggression; but in sport there is action, either vicarious, as with the spectator in a physical contest, or direct; while in art the participation is emotional and no action is called for; the violence exists as a static condition: in comedy it is accepted as funny, in tragedy it is accepted as inevitable.

Emotion is what remains of an intended aggressive activity when it is confined within a reverberating nervous network. Art is that same emotion for which a less destructive outlet has been found, a symbolic artifact in place of an altered circuit. Aggressive activity under the influence of emotion is more apt to be destructive than constructive, whereas art is constructive.

We know that the act of discovery is emotional; because any surprise is stimulating. But why are the best tropes found only in a state of high excitement? It would be instructive perhaps if in searching for an answer to this question we were to find a physiological mechanism. We might learn that cortical channels are sufficiently open so that engrams containing the remotest references can be related through the sudden perception of similarities. Art introduces nothing new into the world except the recognition that there is a sharing of qualities on the part of those material objects which are both spatially remote and functionally different. In the artistic production that might ensue there could occur emotional discharges into harmless and sometimes useful channels. With the knowledge that mechanisms always lie one analytical level below the qualities they produce, the physiological mechanism just described could be responsible for the emergence of the feeling of beauty. Feelings are the expressions of relationships. The feeling of beauty promises security because its effect is to make the spectator feel that he belongs somehow to the world at its most valuable.

The method of art is a variant of the method of inference employed in logical structures. In a first step axioms are established, and this is followed by a drawing of theorems. The axiomatic method may be observed more clearly in those arts which require an interval of time for their complete exposure, such as music, the theatre, or any narrative.

Consider for example Kafka's short story "Metamorphosis." In this tale a young man turns into a cockroach. After his transformation, events around him are treated as ordinary happenings. How does the young man's family behave? Why, in quite conventional ways, made extraordinary by the contrast. The question for his family is, what does one do when a son becomes a cockroach? Here we can see clearly the impossible, contrary-to-fact, imaginatively constructed axioms, and then the detailed journalistic reporting of the theorematic subsequent events. Given a set of imaginative axioms, the rest follows as a sequence of rigorous logical deductions.

In other words, the artist imagines how things could be different from what they are in a way which he finds illuminating. Then he reproduces in some chosen material what he has imagined, thus making the products of his imagination, and hence also the illumination, available to others. It is the same whether he works in musical sounds, sculptural forms, or linguistic expressions, the work of art which results is a delusional system we are pleased to live in for a while. Art is no substitute for ordinary existence but makes up a kind of commentary on it, and by resting us in another world helps us to bear the ugly and the painful parts of our lives.

Art is the domain in which for the purpose of constructing a world of sheer delight all facts are temporarily false and all theories provisionally true. Consistency is the only criterion in art, not completeness: qualitative axioms, qualitative theorems, all move us in the general direction of the concrete. A good illustration of the queer nature of art logic is contained in the question of how a great artist can get away with the espousal of a false philosophy in a true art. I think D. H. Lawrence did just that. In a superb series of novels, he advanced the theory that the irrational is stronger than the rational, that the sex of primitives is more vigorous than the sex of civilized man. Evidently, a false philosophy can be maintained explicitly with considerable success provided only that there is a more valid true philosophy in the work itself, even though it is one which is never allowed to come to the surface.

Evidently, the artist is able to profess one philosophy while working from another. The working philosophy is realism; the professed philosophy is the prevailing one, and it is this one which the artist thinks he accepts. The philosophy in either case only provides the background, for art is a personal product. It is more of a personal product than science, for instance. If one scientist had not discovered a particular law, another would have; and the occurrence of simultaneous discoveries in science is very common. But if

Homer had not written *The Iliad,* Shakespeare *Hamlet* or Mozart the *Requiem Mass,* it is extremely doubtful whether these masterpieces would have been written.

In this highly individual sense art is a power drive which puts us into immediate contact with possible worlds by symbolizing some of the alternative arrangements of the elements of this actual world. It has been laid down in logic that a false proposition materially implies all propositions. This is correct of course, and it enables us to distinguish between what might be just any false propositions and those special false propositions which go into the making of works of art. An artistic false proposition is one which formally implies only those propositions which are consistent with it. Why for instance do tragic *values* seem cosmic when tragic *facts* do not? The answer is that art is the hopeful side of existence, no matter how it is presented.

And that hopeful side takes many forms of expression. Some go beyond the false proposition to an expression by means of what for want of a better term might be described as anti-beauty. The term is not intended to have the same reference as the more familiar term, ugliness. It functions as a kind of counter-beauty, designed for its overpowering effects. The best examples can be taken from the work of the Aztecs and Mayans and from pre-Columbian art generally, where the grotesque presents almost a mirror-image of beauty. The strength of such art is not gained without some expense, such as the loss of detail. Compare it with an art at the other extreme. For an illustration we may consider the paintings of Andrew Wyeth, in which there is sentiment in place of emotion, considerable attention to parts, and consequently no sense of the whole. There is great technical dexterity, yet clear evidence that expertise will never replace insight.

For sentiment is one kind of feeling and emotion another. A work of art, we must remind ourselves at this point, is an artifact constructed by human individuals with a view to arousing certain feelings in themselves and their kind, especially the feeling of sublimity, as Longinus named it. The specific feelings called out by successful works of art are those of the permanence of relatedness, where the relatedness is found to be naturally-occurring: those relations especially which exist in and between material objects. It is not yet clear why harmony in a material object, usually the artistic variety of artifact, can give rise to harmony in the person, expressed as a feeling. The quality of the atmosphere in which men will live henceforth is being designed today by those who are responsible for contemporary works of art.

The aesthetic experience *sui generis* is the satisfaction of feeling the quality of the unity of the world as concentrated in the quality of its symbolic counterpart. Back of this of course is the basic structure itself: that certain combinations of matter are capable of arousing in the human individual a deep and pleasurable emotional response: for example the sculptured forms discovered by Phidias, the selections of sounds chosen by Bach, the arrangement of human situations and words designed by Shakespeare. Has anyone ever asked himself what it means to build into an artifact the stimulus to extremes of feelings, and in particular those feelings that are both pleasurable and reassuring?

Feelings and emotions together with ideas, when involved as reflexes in the reverberating circuit, produce works of art (artifacts). Such feelings are also responses to stimuli from the external world in which qualities as well as relations already exist. Art as the effort to deepen feeling is another way of understanding, or of finding reliance on being. The self-conditioning by artifacts makes possible a deeper penetration of the external world.

Art has not yet caught up with the scientific expansion of our knowledge of nature. It has limited itself thus far to the range available to the unaided senses. The physical sciences have disclosed to us two strange worlds which lie on opposite sides of the familiar world of our common experience: the world of the very small, of atoms and below, and the world of the very large, of galaxies and above. If one of the functions of art is the celebration of existence, here are two directions in which science has opened up to art the new knowledge of hitherto unknown material objects: the more we know about the universe the more there is to celebrate. The artists of the future should be able to range wider and experience more, and so produce works of art more powerful than any we have yet seen. It is possible with some penetration to find cosmic qualities in great abundance and profusion lying on both sides of us and only waiting to be brought into the organization of works of art.

There are signs already of a restlessness of spirit which no longer wishes to feel itself confined. Consider as evidence the struggle of the painters of the non-representational and the abstract schools. Consider the direction which Lipchitz is trying to give sculpture in a new dimension by trying to bring out the internal surfaces. But the artist is not yet prepared to respond to the new experiences which have been made available by the new artifacts, to the photographs taken with the electron microscope and the optical telescope. It is clear that thus far although he has seen them he does not yet feel them and has not become properly excited by them.

And yet they open the doors to entire landscapes of novelty. It has long been known in neurophysiology that monotony of input means loss of consciousness. The nighttime automobile driver who gets no relief from the ribbon of straight road which feeds continually into his vision falls asleep. Artists save us from this kind of retreat with their fresh discoveries and inventions, but artists are rare and it is the social institutions which furnish the familiar environment. The institutions preserve the artistic discoveries of the past and can only survive by imposing them upon us. Perhaps it is only through institutions that we can survive as members of society, but thanks to them we have to fight conventions all the way. Dali, the painter, wrote somewhere that the first man to draw a mermaid was an artist, the second man was a bureaucrat. Due to the mental effects of monotony, beginning with the loss of consciousness and ending with some kind of cultural death, it is important to look to the artist to breathe fresh life into the material environment of society.

The faculty of imagination which the artist possesses makes of him a creature in some sense set apart from society although serving as an essential part of it. But the career of the artist is almost never satisfactory. Where he wants the most to belong he is the most excluded, for his divergence from the ways of others is taken seriously by them. The artist is a highly organized person, an intense individual who enjoys but who also suffers to a greater degree than ordinary people. Then too there is almost always the necessity of humbling himself before such people because of the superior force of economic and political power. He must pretend to acknowledge himself inferior while knowing his work to be superior, a paradox of attitudes which runs right through his entire life. When he is praised or blamed it is nearly always for the wrong reasons.

But when he is at work everything for him seems to come right again. He enjoys the originative process with its ecstatic moments of insight and he is producing something outside himself that will stand without him. The work of art seems to the artist to grow in his presence. As he sits before it each day and connects himself up with it, the increase continues. What he is doing is tying into his unconscious mind the lines from the unfinished work, from the armature, the canvas, the music paper, the typewriter, and then turning on the switch so that the current can flow. Every day there is a little more, until the design is completed. To do this the artist must either know the rules of his art well enough not to regard them as confining or make up his own rules because they seem to him channels of freedom. He recognizes intuitively that the activity of art production must not acknowledge the limitations of rules as such, only their permissiveness, and this is how rules must be treated in producing original art.

Working in this way the artist feels free, and he *is* free within cultural limits because he is unaware of them. Conformity is not imposed, it is rather a cultural secretion which has its effects through the efforts of individual artists to keep up with the work of their contemporaries. In this way the artist is bound by his interests to follow the fashions of his society, to explore the possibilities of his culture. He follows the trends in art as strictly as he would if they were imposed on him by a rigid political dictatorship. The shifts occur at the center, which is usually (though not always) in some capital city.

Art takes us back to the primitive core of unmarked being and is to that extent anti-cultural. Like science, art can flourish in different cultures even though it behaves in each somewhat differently from the way it does in the others. Unlike its companion institutions, however, such as religions and governments, for art there is no conflict involved. This is the institutional advantage of art, that there is no disastrous conflict, only a mutual diffusing of the richness of difference. For art is nature seen from a particular cultural perspective.

The perspective changes with changes in the culture, and these are saltatory. Sharp breaks with the past can be shown to have been derived from the past, but they are, after all, sharp breaks. The various arts of an epoch have a family resemblance which comes from having the same rise and fall. Much of what looks like advance because it is so general throughout the culture may be no more than symptoms of a cultural decline. It was a better world for art, when in classic Greece and the Italian Renaissance children learned from adults, than it is now when, as shown by Klee and Dubuffet, adults learn from children.

The arts of a culture have more in common with each other than any one art has with that same art in other cultures. Just as certain organs serve the somatic organism (the heart, the endocrine glands, the autonomic nervous system), so some institutions serve society internally (the law courts, the police), while others look outside (the sciences, the religions, the arts). It is the paradox of art that while deep in the culture and falling in line with the leading institution, it yet can manage to some extent to be trans-cultural.

Those who live in a culture and partake of its benefits must also pay its price. The artist is often called on not as a citizen merely but as an artist to engage in political action, to take a partisan stand. No doubt there are times when such action seems called for. And yet it is not possible both to engage in the defense of political liberties and to do those things in whose name and for whose sake the political liberties are defended; no man can be both a political actionist and a devoted artist. What a loss it would have been if Bach had spent half his time in practical politics or if Rousseau had spent all of his composing music. True, many contemporary novelists try to disclose how things really are behind the misleading facade of morality and culture. But to the extent that such efforts show in their novels they prove themselves to be indifferent novelists and their writings imperfect novels. Garcia Lorca might have been of more value to his country in the long run if instead of dying for it he had written his poems in exile.

The artist has a social role to play, and he plays it best when he plays it professionally. He is not at odds with those of his predecessors whose work made the culture what it is but he is with those who cannot administer the culture without accepting its values as fundamental and irreplaceable. The keepers of the culture regard themselves and their role as proprietary. But the artist renews the culture despite the best efforts of its advocates to prevent him. Art is not an entertainment merely, although in a popular sense it is also that; but it is more than that: an intensification of life. The country without the refreshment of a new and living art is in danger of becoming the background for a social milieu limited to individual stereotypical behavior—its messages without meaning, its symbols without significance, its pleasures without enhancement. Art is a joyful but also a serious business, and not the mere rest period it tends to become in the midst of the successes of a scientific-industrial culture.

PART THREE
Theory

EIGHT

Art: A Definition and
Some Consequences

For a long while it has been recognized that among those who alter materials with a view to making useful things the artist occupies a special place. For the things that he makes if he is a great artist are cherished and returned to again and again. They are among the most valued possessions of the human species.

There are periods, however, when such eminence is acknowledged to hold for past artists but not for present ones. At the outset of our scientific age the artist was derogated as a man whose achievements were poor when compared with the wonders of science. What is a painting or a musical score compared with an airplane or a television set? How can any theory of prosody offer as much interest as a new theorem in quantum mechanics? But the artist was hardly one to accept such a judgment, nor indeed did he have to. Unfortunately, but understandable in such a case, his proponents fought back by exaggerating his claims. He was, they insisted, the greatest wonder worker of all, for he spun his works of art out of his inner spiritual resources. He was a creator of art, and (it was implied if not said) as such second only to the Creator of the universe.

In such a way does the pendulum swing, crossing the truth unnoticed on its way to extreme falsehoods. But there were already on hand older views of art which did not square with these exaggerations. There was for instance the conception of art as discovery, the method of assembling materials which themselves were already present, and there was the conception of art as invention, a version which seems to lie halfway between creation and discovery. A good illustration of the first might be a Schumann etude for the piano, and of the second a mobile by Alexander Calder.

We shall not need to deal with invention here for it begs the question posed by the two views which are the most at odds. Is art a creation or a discovery? The currently accepted phrase, "creative art," clearly implies the former, as though the artist were a god and the work of art his creature. The arguments for this position are many and they have been well aired. I would like therefore to speak for the latter conception, namely, that the artist does not create art but discovers it.

Instead of defending the position abstractly, let us look at what actually happens in the production of a work of art. The simplest example might be taken from piano music, for the range of material available to the artist is here at its most restricted. Built into the piano (perhaps by accident because it is nothing more than a keyed dulcimer, just as the dulcimer itself had been nothing more than a hammered psaltery) and thereafter brought along with the possibilities which make it available as a musical instrument, are certain necessary limitations. Working within these limitations has been a price the composer and performer have been happy to pay for the range of the possibilities. The composer for the piano has at his disposal all of the black and white notes of seven octaves. He may use each of these as often and as long as he wishes, and his score is a record of some of his preferences. The length to which the notes are held and the frequency with which they are struck are the results of his own free choice. All of the notes available to the composer were already there as parts of the piano. Indeed he makes a selection from among the many permutations and combinations which the construction of the instrument has provided. He selects, nothing more. Yet let it not be supposed that this in any way implies the derogation of the composer. Very few musicians since Chopin have been able to choose as well as he. Genius is genius no less because the artist is a discoverer and not a creator.

The difference between the professional and the amateur composer is that the music of the professional is apt to be more interesting and even more beautiful, more specifically, interesting because more beautiful than the music of the amateur. They use the same notes, notes of the same duration and frequency, but not in the same order, and this makes all of the difference between music and noise. The choice available to both is the same, but the professional is able to choose more significantly. Amateurs are at liberty to do whatever the professionals do, and it is only the force of the result which counts. I have on occasion written a fugue or two, and I use the same little black marks on ruled paper that J. S. Bach used. But somehow the differences in our selections make mine unspeakably trivial and his a joy forever. I will not ask why this has to be so, although certainly it is a crucial question; I will not ask because at the present time no one knows the answer. If someone did know, we could at will educate artists to be geniuses, and we cannot.

What I have said about music could be said equally for any of the other arts. As with music, all of the possibilities are there, but it takes a genius to make a supremely significant selection. A painter can choose any of the infinite number of colored shapes within the limits self-prescribed by the selection of the size of his canvas. The stonecutter chips away the parts he does not want, the sculptor in clay adds what he needs where he thinks he needs it. Shakespeare used words which were current in the English language in his time. Other choices could have been made, but none were made as happily. The result of his faculty for selecting is that we have all been indebted to him for his gift to us ever since.

It is clear that the artist shapes his material with a view to capturing in it some of the values to which the appreciator of art can react emotionally in a special way. In what way I have tried to show elsewhere; what is important here is that the work of the artist is objective and constructive. He alters his material in order to give it a certain shape, for it is the shape which is to carry the value and have the effect. The important thing to note at this point is that shaped material is material even though it is shaped. And whatever shape it is given is one of the shapes which it potentially could be given.

A work of art is a material thing, and no less so because there are other kinds of material things. It is a material thing with a difference, for it has been carefully contrived with a particular end in view. Nothing entered it from that intangible stuff which allegedly composes the artist's soul: he did not spin out the work of art or project it from his inner consciousness. It is a work of art chiefly because, due to the singular properties of his insight into matter, he knew what kind of selection to make; nothing personal in any final sense, nothing subjective, except an intuition on the part of the artist of the potential properties of the material provided certain alterations are made in it.

The artist, then, is a man who has the talent for significantly altering material things, for symbolically arranging sequences of sound waves which already existed, or for putting together colored shapes which he found ready to hand in the world. It is, obviously enough, a talented individual who does this, and the talented individual is in every case a human being. Art is the work of man, no doubt of that, and nothing that I have been saying about interpreting the artistic process as discovery is intended to cancel the importance of the role played in it by the artist.

There is, in short, no disposition in this argument to evade the significance of the fact that art is man-made. Works of art do not occur spontaneously but only after immense effort on the part of an artist. Without the artist there would be no art, and so the artist may consider himself an important member of society and his products precious to its members. It is not necessary to believe the artist a creator in order to hold a view of his function. If he is a successful discoverer that is enough. What he actually does do in either case is enough; and he does the same thing, only the interpretation is different. Ordinarily, those who glorify the role of the artist prefer the interpretation of him as creator. But it is the point here that this preference is not compulsory. Even if he is held to be merely a discoverer, one has only to remember that there are always few such discoverers.

I take it that on the basis of this conception the term, "artist," need not necessarily be an honorific one. It is rather a generic term, and includes all those who professionally engage in the production of works of art. No assumption of eminence ought to be implied, however, since numerically the evidence runs very much the other way: not every artist is a great artist. Many are called but few are chosen.

The artist has been for so long the underdog of societies, ranking well below the financially and the politically influential, that he tends to compensate by making exaggerated claims for himself. Granted that there is no human enterprise as ambitious or as enriching for humanity as art, it does not follow that every fellow who calls himself an artist necessarily justifies the claim to greatness which unquestionably must be bestowed on the genius. For the answer to an underevaluation ought not to be a permanent overevaluation. A visit to the nearest gallery exhibiting contemporary paintings will confirm this statement. A glance at a few of our recent public monuments will convince anyone with taste that the Greeks were happier in their favored sculptors.

Ours is a great period in artistic experimentation, but it may prove to be not quite so great in artistic achievement. Some innovations mark definite advances, others are worthless; and it is not easy to tell readily with which we are dealing. One of the values of any abstract consideration of aesthetic values is that it enables contemporaries to take a longer and more detached look at the artistic efforts of their day and to anticipate the eventual evaluations which may fall to it. For in dealing with the supreme efforts of man—with the arts, as well as the sciences and the philosophies—it is necessary to balance neatly, like a tightrope walker, between the concrete and the abstract, between the temporary and the permanent. It is my contention here that the very topic we have been discussing should lead us to comparisons which will reveal certain of the weaknesses inherent in modern art.

Two points have thus far been firmly established, I hope. The first is the material nature of art production. The second is the necessity for human agency. Art has here been declared a discovery of some of the more significant formal properties of matter rather than a creation spun out of the soul of the artist. But the fact remains that they are the result of the work of the artist, who continues to be indispensable.

Clearly our two points must now somehow be fused. And they can be fused in any important way only if they can be united under a definition. The understanding of anything is aided by precise definition, for this is an illumination of a kind. And if we can zero in on a definition that will meet all the requirements ordinarily asked of it, we may have found also an instrument which will help us to solve some problems in criticism.

Let us next, then, approach the question of the definition of art. That art involves beauty essentially few have doubted; and those who doubt prefer "truth" to "beauty." But "truth" is a logical term, not a value, and whatever art is or is not it certainly does involve value. There is such a thing as truth-value, but this too is a complicated idea which I have endeavored to treat in another place. So let us here settle for "beauty," and let us remember that we have settled also on the notion of "discovery" rather than "creation." Then art is some kind of discovery of beauty. "Apprehension" may be a better term than "discovery," because apprehension is a kind of physical seizure and involves laying hold of. But we cannot define art as "the apprehension of beauty" pure and simple because this would make an artist of any man who appreciates a sunset. We shall have to add to this definition that the actions of the man are deliberate and that somehow he has managed to alter a material object. Without the term, deliberate, we do not have the man, and without the alteration we do not have the art.

But then if we define art as "the deliberate apprehension of beauty in a material object," we encounter some difficulty with "deliberate" as a necessary qualification. It has been suggested that certain forms which are naturally occurring are authentic works of art, such as some beach stones worn into beautiful shapes by the ebb and flow of the tides, or certain pieces of driftwood grooved by the actions of currents in the rivers on which they have been floating. These, it is argued, were not the work of any artist, yet they have achieved artistic beauty.

If there are naturally occurring works of art, as there are naturally occurring veins of silver and deposits of uranium, then art cannot be the result only of deliberate effort. If non-human nature is capable of producing works of art then human agency is obviously not definite. The apprehension of beauty, one might almost say the occurrence of beauty, in a material object would be quite enough to enable it to be considered a work of art.

It would be possible to reduce to absurdity the defenders

of the artistic merits of smooth beach stones and worn driftwood by asking why anything to be a work of art had to be small and resembling the works of art made by human artists. Why is not a mountain a work of art, or a sunset? Geology will disclose that over the millennia something has been altered in the surface contours of the earth to make the mountain, and meteorology will disclose that in the last few hours the water content of the atmosphere has been altered to reflect the sunlight. But then the argument reduces to the contention that anything in nature is a work of art, and art becomes a synonym for nature.

Clearly then we are in no position to use the term, art, in connection with natural beauty or to regard as works of art the products which man has had no hand in the making. It is not possible to show objectively that a subject was necessary, but until naturally occurring Mozart symphonies and Homeric epics are found the contention will have to stand. We need to abandon this line of argument therefore and return to our definition. But we have gained something from it nonetheless. For the argument raises an interesting question in connection with contemporary art, and actually has more significance than the issues which occasioned it. I propose to look into some of these deeper meanings.

There is no doubt that some contemporary artists have produced works of art which are close to what are called natural forms, forms which are naturally occurring in the non-human world; the sculpture of Hans Arp, the paintings and drawings of Paul Klee, for instance. But these are simpler than, say, the sculptures of Phidias or the paintings of Velasquez. There are no naturally occurring Phidian forms, no naturally occurring Velasquezian forms.

For these the intervention of the human artist has been and evidently continues to be necessary. What Arp and Klee have tried to do, evidently, is to produce works of art which could have occurred without them. But what an odd ambition! How very different from the ambition of Phidias or Velasquez! Can such very divergent aims be claimed equally for the artistic process?

What are we to conclude from this distinction? A number of points could certainly be made, but for our purposes one seems more important than the others. We may understand that the contemporary artist is dangerously close to non-human nature, close to demonstrating that in art human nature is unnecessary. But there is something wrong here. For cultural achievements consist in the main in material things altered through human agency in ways which tend to make them more amenable to human uses. It is human to *see* the beautiful in nature—all men are capable of such insights; but it is artistic to *make* art out of nature, to make material things more specifically beautiful as works of art. The further from non-human nature the artist is able to take his material, the more he is apt to produce an authentic work of art. From this point of view Arp and Klee are only imitators of nature, while Phidias and Velasquez are artists.

There is a difference, even though what all four men produced may be valuable. For what the artist seeks to do is to enhance the naturally occurring beauty which he finds everywhere. Nature is inherently beautiful, though it is not true for everything in nature that the beauty lies on the surface and is immediately evident. A work of art is a material object so constructed that despite its complexity the leading edge of its interest is set to move in the direction of its beauty. It serves no other purpose, it has no other intent, it can yield no other comprehensive interpretation.

The separation between naturally occurring forms and works of art is a dim one with a vague borderline, but it exists nonetheless. For dusk and dawn do not cancel the sharpness of the difference between noon and midnight. The distinction itself rests on the degree of complexity: works of art are usually far more complex than naturally occurring forms. Complexity is the necessary but not the sufficient cause of powerful qualitative effects. A Bach fugue is more powerful than a simple melody, however lovely the melody; and the reason is the force that piles up from complex relationships. Of course it is possible to have the complexity without the qualitative power, but it is not possible to have the qualitative power without the complexity.

Perhaps we can account for the importance of the difference between naturally occurring forms and works of art by approaching it from another perspective. Let us begin by recalling the well known opposition of nature and man. Man, in this sense, has somehow been held to stand apart from nature and to some extent even at odds with it. What warrant is there for accepting this? In the empirical hierarchy in which biological organisms are complex developments of lower chemical structures, the separation of man from nature seems unjustifiable. In what in the philosophy of science are called the integrative levels, there is an unbroken chain of increasing complexity from atom through molecule and cell to organism and man. It is not derogatory to call man, then, a natural animal even though it must be admitted that he has powers superior to the other animals, powers which consist, however, chiefly in his control of the material part of his environment.

THEORY

The distinction between the human-natural (for all that is human is natural) and the non-human-natural (an awkward phrase for what is ordinarily designated as nature) is a subtle and difficult one. If human beings are natural animals (and what animal is not natural?) and if culture always includes a material component which consists in some material which has been altered through human agency for a special purpose, then works of art are the products of what natural animals have done to natural materials. They are somehow on the dividing line between the human-natural and the non-human-natural and belong to a third category. A work of art is—whatever else it is—a material which has been altered through the agency of the artist who had a specific reason for so doing. This end was not necessarily accomplished by altering the material so that the result appeared to be something which could have occurred without him. Such a negative aim, however modest, would have an import at odds with the aesthetic; it would mean that the artist would regard himself as an artist but his art as superfluous. He would, if he is right, have nothing to do except to search on beaches and by riversides for works of art which nature had constructed without him.

But this point of view is a recent phenomenon and, needless to add, it has not been followed to such a logical conclusion. Art has traditionally involved large-scale alterations. As a matter of fact, there have been no naturally occurring Parthenons or Bach fugues, and there are not likely to be. No one is going to come upon a *Macbeth* untouched by human hands or a landscape that did not require alterations by a Monet or a Gauguin in order to become a work of art. Such works of art are, as we are wont to say, far removed from nature; by which we mean, of course, far removed from that state of nature in which humans have not interfered. When they do interfere the result is unique, and nothing like it is found otherwise in nature.

The repudiation of the production of works of art similar to naturally occurring forms as a preferential method to be pursued by the artist has important consequences which bear on the evaluation of certain aspects of the contemporary art movement. What we have here, among other thoughts, is an implied negative criticism of the elemental and primitive forms of modern art. The modern artist has set himself the task of imitating non-human, naturally occurring forms, and this imitation is bound to be derivative and secondary. It is a falsely conceived goal which he cannot hope to attain: man striving to be other than man, endeavoring to contribute to art through the slavish imitation of non-art. Man, that complex natural product, may be able to *improve* upon what nature does without his aid, but what he does will never be the *same* as what nature does in that way.

One cannot help but wonder how and why he got himself into such an embarrassing and awkward predicament. It would seem as though the modern artist has made a problem for himself that no classical artist ever made: he has selected to compete with non-human nature on its own terms. And this competition he cannot ever hope to win. No wonder that he finds his artistic sympathies and parallels in the arts of primitive and even of prehistoric man! The more sophisticated art of the best periods, the art of the classical Greeks, of the Renaissance Italians, of the Ming Chinese, are foreign to him, as foreign as they are to natural objects which have remained undisturbed by artists.

The contemporary artist, then, plays a dangerous game

of challenging nature by undertaking to construct forms which occur in nature without his help. We have seen that in this way he suggests his own elimination from the world of art. "Creative" art, as a consequence of the turn he has taken, becomes not a creation nor even a construction but a search among natural objects for those particular ones which already possess a high aesthetic quality.

On another front he does construct complicated forms, but when this turns into a struggle to be as non-representational as possible, he succeeds only in imitating nature. "Non-representative" art is not non-representative, it simply (and unintentionally) represents lower forms in non-human nature. Brancusi wanted some of his sculpture to look like eggs, while Jackson Pollock produced canvases which resemble enlargements of some microscopic slides of bacteria and other cellular constituents. It is impossible to find in any work of art a component which cannot be found somewhere in nature. In this sense abstract expressionism produces only the more recondite representations.

It is not difficult to discover what led art down such a blind alley. The key lies perhaps in a misunderstanding of the experimental physical sciences. Science has been a tremendous force, an institution which not only made its own way toward the top of the culture but also deeply disturbed and in many ways changed the contents of other institutions. Now as it happens artists above all people are sensitive to their environment, and art has been profoundly affected by the sciences. The artists have had many different ways of dealing with the effects of science. Many of these ways are based on misunderstandings of it. The assumption for instance that science is chiefly physics, and that the physical is chiefly the simple (in the sense of undisturbed gross objects from the world of the middle-sized as these are found in the purview of the unaided human senses) is obviously false. Both the instruments employed in making observations and experiments and the findings which result from these possess an intricacy unknown to the most involved art. Nature is immensely complex, and the disclosures of some of these immense complexities has been one result of the investigations conducted by the empirical sciences.

In following the primitive, the basic, and the elemental, the artists have not only mistaken the accomplishments of science, but, far worse: they have been led down the wrong artistic path. In so doing they have all but read themselves out of their rightful place in the human enterprise. Art should stand on its own feet as an institution and not be obliged to derive the ground of its authenticity from others. The institution of science may have *dis*placed other institutions, it has not *re*placed them. Art supplies a need not supplied by science, and it should not look to science for its guidelines.

Not all modern artists are guilty of such an erroneous turn toward undisturbed nature. Cézanne and Van Gogh could hardly be called naturalists, yet their canvases resemble nothing so much as interpretations of nature, nature altered through the agency of the supreme views of authentic artists. Cézanne's landscapes have been compared with photographs of the originals, and it is clear that he made selected changes for aesthetic reasons, with what can only be called astonishingly successful results. Nature for the genuine artist is the source of his raw material, not only the paints and canvas surfaces, the clay or stone, but also the forms which are naturally occurring. In this sense there are no forms in art which do not occur somewhere in nature, and so there are no forms which are not naturally occurring. What the artist does is to select the forms that he wants from among those which are available to him in his natural environment. These he puts together in new ways with a view to the aesthetic effect of the whole. In a word, he selects familiar parts and reassembles them to produce a new whole.

The new whole is an original work of art which he alone had the insight to perceive as a possibility. His genius lay in his ability to make alterations in the material object which covered it, to disclose it, to lay it bare on the surface so that others could share his pleasure by perceiving actually what it is that he saw potentially. Nature is far richer than its superficial appearances, and its possibilities are almost endless. It is the contribution of the artist that he is able to find his way among these endless possibilities to the few which are meaningful in the particular way which we call aesthetic. He is able to elicit enough to justify his tremendous efforts, his technical skills and his intuitive perceptions. He is, then, a discoverer and not a creator, a researcher if you like, and not an inventor, an artist in that special executive sense which the term implies.

NINE

The Truth-Value of Art

I

Our problem in this chapter is the relation of art to truth. In what sense can it be said that a work of art is true, or, for that matter, false? I propose to examine this question in the following pages and if possible to arrive at some definite answers.

It will be best to begin the investigation by repeating a few definitions. I define art as the deliberate apprehension of beauty in a material object. I define beauty as the quality which emerges from the perfect relations of parts in a whole. Beauty of course is one of the values. Another is goodness; still another is truth. Since our aim is to determine something of the truth-value of art, we shall need finally a definition of truth. Truth can be defined in two ways. I accept the conventional definitions of truth according to correspondence or coherence, the correspondence between propositions and the objects to which they refer, and the coherence or consistency of parts in a whole, respectively. By a truth-value is meant any truth which corresponds to an underlying value.

What does it mean then to talk about the truth-value of a work of art? For this it will be necessary to consider the work of art as a form of communication. The work of art, it is often asserted, says something, though what it says is qualitative rather than quantitative, and it is said connotatively rather than denotatively. All communication is about something but it is not necessarily to somebody. It communicates to a perspective which presumably somebody could occupy, but it is equally communication when the perspective is unoccupied. A sign is no less a sign during that interval when there is nobody to read it.

In the case of a work of art the communication is indirect and even when the work itself is a literary work it cannot be put into words. The moral or the meaning of a novel, a poem, or a play is as difficult to express directly, didactically and denotatively as the meaning of a painting or of an orchestral composition. It will be impossible to describe in any particular instance simply because qualities cannot be described. The meaning of a painting no more lends itself to exact description than does the taste of an orange or the sight of a color. But if we cannot describe the truth-value of works of art in particular, we can do so in general. We can say something perhaps which will help in understanding what sort of value the truth-value of art is.

II

Like all other material objects, the work of art is a whole

consisting of parts. It is a new whole of old parts. Although the whole has existed in no other context, this is not true of the parts. The artist imagines how things could be, and projects his imaginings in a material object constructed in order to serve them. He is assisted in this project by his observations of how things are. What he actually does is to select certain material which may be parts of other objects and reassemble them in an art object, which deserves that name because unlike other objects it has a high representative value as a sign of quality. The unicorn belongs to the fictive world but its rhinoceros' horn and its horse's body do not. A phoenix, we are told, is a bird which arises from the ashes of its own fire. Nobody has ever seen a phoenix, but we are all very familiar with birds, ashes and fires.

Every whole has its qualitative aspect as a whole, but the work of art differs from other wholes in the extent of its qualitative aspect, by the way in which it points to values beyond itself and larger than itself. We all emerge from prolonged exposure to great art with the profound reassurance of ultimate belonging. Everything is a part of the universe, but in the work of art this participation is made manifest indirectly.

Now it is another peculiarity of works of art that such indirect reference is mediated by a direct reference to some actual thing or event. For instance, the *Oresteia* trilogy refers to the universe via the succession of a royal family in Greece. The *B-Minor Mass* of Bach does so via a Lutheran Church service. The object in the case of an abstract expressionist painting by Jackson Pollock is a uniform whole of order consisting of actual parts of colored shapes. The object here is a fictive object but the parts are actual parts: we have all seen curves and colors of this character. All works of art have the same ultimate reference which is the beauty of the universe, but an intermediate is necessary, and the intermediate is made axiologically referential by means of the work of art. This is its communicative value, that it points in effect to the significance of something else.

There is then the work of art itself, the object to which it refers directly, and the value of the universe to which it refers indirectly. If A is the work of art, B the object to which it refers directly and C the value of the universe, then A implies that B implies C. More precisely, A implies the implication of C by B rather than either B itself or C itself. The work of art, that is, implies a value rather than an object though it does so by means of an object.

Now the object to which the work of art refers directly need not be an obvious one in all cases. The object, in the case of the *Oresteia* trilogy is more obvious than it is in the *B-Minor Mass* and in the *B-Minor Mass* it is more obvious than it is in a painting by Jackson Pollock. An abstract object, however, is no less an object. The sounds selected by Bach and the colored shapes selected by Pollock all exist, and to have assembled them in a new way is to have made a new object but an object nonetheless. To make a unity of parts assembled by selection from other objects in which they did not exist together is to make a unity nonetheless, and every unity is a whole in this sense.

There are many direct objects to which art may refer, as many objects in fact as there are works of art. But there is only one indirect and secondary reference, since there is only one universe of value. Thus various works of art constitute as many indirect references to the axiological universe, some weak, others strong, and a few so overpowering that we seem through their appreciation to be immediately in the presence of that universe itself and suffused with an enveloping sense of value which tends to obliterate everything else, all shortcomings and difficulties, all limitations and frustrations.

Thus there is always an object where there is a work of art. There is an object corresponding to the *Oresteia* trilogy and another corresponding to the *B-Minor Mass*, and there is an object corresponding to the Pollock picture no less because in each of these cases there is a fictive object rather than an actual object. Now a fictive object is a peculiar kind of possible object, possible because non-contradictory and composed of actual parts. We can see the narrow and indefinite band which separates fictive reality from possibility on the one side and from actuality on the other. It can be shown, in fact, that the object to which a work of art refers is always a possible object but that this does not mean never an actual object. We shall have to ask in this connection whether it is always the case that a work of art which is true of a peculiar kind of possible object called a fictive object is always false of an actual object, whether in a work artistic truth is always possible truth and never actual truth, and whether we are justified in using truth in the first place is such a connection, whether, in short, there can be artistic truth unless there can also be artistic falsehood. For if there is no such thing as artistic falsehood then the term *truth* in the phrase "*artistic truth*" is out of place.

III

The study of systems is in its infancy. There are many kinds of systems, but we shall be dealing here only with two, and these may be named the logical and the axiological, after the two typical ways in which they have been chiefly employed. We shall have to consider both in connection with works of art. The first is the linear type of logico-mathematical system whose consistency rests on certain assumptions called axioms from which deductions, called theorems, follow. The second type is the system which consists in the integration of parts in a whole. The linear system is best illustrated for works of art by the theme-and-variation type of musical composition, as for instance in the classic fugue. The circular system is best illustrated by an easel painting or a portrait bust, in which the unity is integral and there is no starting point. The first type of system is linear and relational, the second type circular and qualitative. We shall see that although the proofs of systems or the evidence for their truth is logically irrelevant to their nature as logical systems, it is still the case that truth by correspondence is peculiar to linear systems of the first type and truth by coherence is peculiar to circular systems of the second type.

Let us begin by considering an example of the first type of system as incorporated in a literary work of art. A literary work of any length requires a lapse of time for its unfolding. It has a consistency which rests on certain assumptions, stated at or near the outset, from which all else appears as consequences. In the case of *Hamlet*, for instance, a number of propositions could be formulated which the audience is asked to accept at least *pro tem*, and it is asked to accept them as though it believed in their truth. We can enumerate a few as follows: Hamlet was a prince in Denmark; His uncle had murdered his father; His uncle had married his mother; Hamlet wished to avenge his father's murder, etc. These are so to speak the axioms of the system. Given the axioms, it is the case that the theorems follow logically; that is to say, they are deducible from the axioms; so that we are entitled to talk about the axiomatic *Hamlet* propositions and the theorematic events of the play. The various speeches and actions of the characters in *Hamlet* convey other sentiments which may be regarded as propositions on the move, and these propositions, more numerous than the axioms, are the theorems of the system. The dénouement corresponds to the logical conclusions of the system.

As a play *Hamlet* is the account of certain events which (according to the play itself) took place at the court of Denmark. Factually it is reasonable to suppose that they never happened, are not happening, and presumably never will happen. But when the play is given we are asked as we watch them happen to believe for the time being that they are happening, and the play is given again and again. What, then, is the truth-value of the account. Is it true or false? More specifically, is it absolutely true, absolutely false, true or false in some degree, or indeterminate?

As is the case with any other logical structure, the play is true if the assumptions are accepted. If credence is to be granted the *Hamlet* propositions, then the events recorded about them follow with logical consistency. But to assert truth in terms of consistency is only to say that the play possesses unity, that the *Hamlet* propositions and their consequences in action are non-contradictory. But now let us turn to the question of truth. Here the issue is clear: the *Hamlet* propositions are not true. There never was a prince in Denmark named Hamlet, whose father was murdered by an uncle who then married his widow and became king in his place. Can we then say they are false? Are they contrary to fact?

The answer of course is that they are. But is this sufficient warrant to describe them as false? A proposition contrary to fact may be said to be false when and only when it
asserts its own (factual) truth. But do the *Hamlet* propositions assert their own factual truth? This is the question on
which the whole issue of the truth-value of art turns. And it
seems to me that they do. That is to say, they assert truth by
correspondence but not correspondence with fact, correspondence instead with a kind of surrogate fact, a factual
generality qualitatively expressed. For the facts to which
such surrogate art corresponds are tangential to what we
should ordinarily call facts; they are the symbolic assertions
which correspond with the qualities of possible facts. We
are having to deal here with the consistency of a world made
of fact-like things and events but still one not making the
claim to factual truth in the ordinary and literal sense. And
so the *Hamlet* propositions cannot be said to be false to
what we ordinarily call fact any more than they can be said
to be true of it.

A fact is any segment of existence sufficiently integral to
allow it to be considered in isolation from the rest of existence. A description of such a segment is a statement about a
fact. The statement is perforce as limited as the fact it pur-
ports to encompass. But while statements about fact are
inherently limited, the facts themselves are not. Contained
in existence are not only particulars but also their qualities
and relations, and it can be either of these to which reference is made in a statement about fact. If the reference is to
a quality, then the statement can only communicate it indirectly by means of the reference of language but can communicate it directly if made in some material capable of
supporting qualities. The *Hamlet* propositions contain

indirect references, while the Bach references contain the qualities themselves.

There are further difficulties, for we have been talking about reference to actual fact. But there is such a thing also as reference to possible fact. When we talk about the truth or falsity of propositions, we mean in reference to fact. The propositions are said to be descriptions of fact (or not). But when we say they are not, the relevance is still to fact. The universe of discourse remains that of actuality and the propositions describe or fail to describe actual situations. But in the case of works of art, it will be contended here, the universe of discourse is shifted. The propositions of works of art, both those which serve as axioms and those which serve as theorems, refer to possible objects rather than to actual objects; possible, that is to say, in the sense that they could have happened but did not, not in the sense that they will happen but have not.

The world of fact, of material objects in action and reaction, consists in things and events, but these contain their own qualities and relations, or, in other words, exhibit logic and value. The fact-world for art purposes is the world of fact insofar as it contains values; the facts for art are the value-facts. *True* for art therefore means correspondence with value.

The imaginary world of the artist—perhaps it would be less misleading to say of the work of art—is the epistemological world because it was constructed of images from the subjective perspective in which they were selected from actual objects. The fictive world of art stands therefore in a tangential relation to the actual world, abstracting from it a selection of its values, and not of all its values, not the values of the good, for instance, but only the values of the beautiful. The selection has as its goal a more beautiful arrangement of parts in the whole than can be found in the parts of those wholes which go to make up the actual world as the artist finds it. He reconstructs it nearer to its representation of the values of the universe, and in order to make the latter more telling does this in a special set of actual objects called works of art.

What bearing does the controversy over counterfactual conditionals have on this position? I should say none directly. For counterfactual conditionals are in direct reference to fact; they are as their name suggests contrary to fact. But the *Hamlet* propositions are not asserting fact and are neither true nor false of it; they are not related to fact in this way. But that they are related to fact in some way can hardly be denied. It is no less genuine for being indirect. Art relates, but indirectly. The spectator of a good performance of *Hamlet* is illuded at least temporarily. The details of the play are such that he is temporarily persuaded to suppose that he is watching them happen, and this may make such an indelible emotional impression upon him that it can never be altogether erased. He has participated intimately in a fictive world.

Considered in relation to fact the *Hamlet* propositions are a set of false propositions but it is not legitimate to consider them only in this way. Perhaps it would be better to say that counterfactual conditionals have no bearing on the problem of the *Hamlet* propositions but that the problem of the *Hamlet* propositions has a bearing on counterfactual conditionals indirectly. They show that there is more than one kind of counterfactual conditional. There is the kind which runs directly counter to fact, and there is the kind which suggests a possible domain tangential to fact.

The world of fact is a dense world and contains many layers and components. Facts of one sort merge into those of another, until we are confronted with the entire presence of existence as it flows out of the past and into the future.

The great contribution of Bergson to philosophy is his assurance that the domain of existence is richer than any of our limited schemes. It extends both in intensity and in extensity beyond what is disclosed to us by our experience. Art penetrates through the dimension of intensity, and the reality thus laid bare includes the tangential realities of the fictive world. Every logical net we throw in order to encompass existence is a self-selecting device. It contrives to include only what it was designed to cover and thus will contain only certain sorts of facts, those sorts of fact which can either verify or falsify logical propositions linguistically expressed. But there are other sorts of propositions; there are linguistic propositions which are not merely logical in this sense, such as the value propositions, and there are other sorts of propositions which are not linguistically expressed which are also value propositions. Material objects are capable of expressing values and we can see this illustrated in plastic works of art: paintings or sculpture. For plastic works of art have their own propositions as much as do literary works of art. There are the Bach propositions which are musically expressed and the Henry Moore propositions which are sculpturally expressed.

We can make another sort of cut in order to make the point clearer. We can say that truth is a function of space (or of spatial occupancy) and value is a function of time (or of temporal duration). In the time arts the values approach truth in time. With repetition the true values tend to assert themselves. But with the space arts either the value is there or it is not, and nothing that happens will serve to intensify or change it. Anything which occupies space is capable of rendering propositions about fact true or false, and anything which endures over a time is capable of rendering propositions about values true or false. Thus the truth-value of art is easier to detect in the case of those works of art which require time for their unfolding, such as a symphony, a novel, or a play, than it is in the case of those which can be apprehended all at once, such as a painting or a piece of sculpture.

In the time arts, the arts which require time for their unfolding, the effect is cumulative, and only by looking back upon it can the unity which arises from the theorematic consequences having issued from axiomatic first statements become evident. In the space arts, however, the unity makes its appearance as soon as the art itself does. The all-at-onceness of an easel painting or a portrait bust brings the unity to the foreground immediately. It is more difficult in such a case to formulate the axioms as was done much earlier in the study for *Hamlet.* There is another reason for this. The time arts tend to be of the theme-and-variations type. Logical conditions are imposed axiomatically at the outset and the possibilities for integrated beauty explored in the limits prescribed by them. Thus such works of art are linear. The space arts are logically circular; there is no beginning and no end. Thus the whole takes precedence phenomenologically over its parts, whereas in the time arts the parts take phenomenological precedence. Either Rembrandt's beef in the butcher shop presents itself entirely and with all its effectiveness or it does not do so at all. But this is not the case with the *B-Minor Mass.* Generally speaking, the time arts rely upon correspondence primarily whereas the space arts rely upon coherence primarily.

In summary, then, the truth-value of works of art is the truth of value, not the truth of fact. Or, more precisely, facts contain both logical and axiological elements, and it is the former exclusively which logic has seized upon and preempted for its own as though there were no other elements. But facts are not entirely logical and the extra-logical aspect of facts is not the false aspect but the value aspect. The false aspect is a function of propositions exclusively and not of facts: there is no such thing as a false fact. It should be noted here parenthetically that to say that art is extra-logical is not to say that it is illogical. Value has its own shapes, and to say that art is concerned with values is to say that it is concerned with its own forms. Value lies outside the logical, but what is extra-logical is not necessarily illogical, as indeed true art is not. Fact contains both logic and value, and it is the value rather than the logic to which the propositions of art refer. The *Hamlet* propositions refer to value-facts and of these they are true.

Thus when we say that the propositions of art refer to possible objects we mean that they refer to factual objects in their value aspect. A more traditional way of expressing this same assertion would be to say that the work of art is symbolically true. In the conventional usage, a symbol is a word which represents a value, but it has the wrong sort of subjective connotation for the present argument. I am talking about the reference of the proposition to fact and not about the reference of the proposition to what the subject expressing the proposition may have meant it to convey. There is nothing either subjective or mental in the interpretation of the truth-value of art which is here proposed.

We are considering instead the work of art and its relation to such aspects of fact as would render it true or false: the truth-value of art.

IV

Something more of the truth-value of art can be illustrated perhaps if we approach the problem from the perspective of the appreciation of art, always provided of course that the illustrative nature of such a perspective is well understood. For the psychological aspects of art depend upon the existence of art and not the reverse. There are artists and there are appreciators because there is art, and it is not the case that there is art because there are artists and appreciators. Without the artist there might be no art object, but this is a matter of occasion and not of cause. The object of art is the cause of the artist, not the occasion.

Every work of art pretends to some condition of reality wherein there is a transformation of fact into value. The characteristic work of art is that which best presents a myth. The myth is the truth represented by its value; that is why in myth direct reference to the value of the universe is warranted. A myth is a story about the symbolic adventures of personified philosophical categories in which the events are presented as value-facts, in short a qualitative account of reality. We are accustomed to having fact transformed into value by means of the time arts, for the myth always requires time for its unfolding even though the space arts may employ segments consisting in cross-sections cut through it. But such art whatever it portrays is self-contained; it is a unit, having its own integrity and independence. And so it is not surprising that the appreciator of art is asked to get into the world of value-fact of the work of art through the work of art itself and entirely by its means. Appreciation of this sort is not a passive function but a vigorous effort. The appreciator has to be able to offer the most intense and prolonged concentration, an abstraction from his other capabilities of sufficient duration to lift him into the world of the work of art where the immensity of its reference is all-enveloping. When this is accomplished, and during its tenure, the work of art becomes fact-presumptive; that is to say, its world presents itself as the fact world, as the ordinary condition of actuality. There has been an assumption with respect to reality which is essential to the work of art. At this point truth and being are one.

The appreciator who is sufficiently (even though only momentarily) absorbed in the work of art accepts *its* world as *the* world; that is to say, he believes in the truth of the contents of its communication. As a result of its force, he believes that things are as he feels them to be; and even if he is able still to look outside the art a little, he still believes that the art is how things are *essentially*. In the contact with the value-facts of art the appreciator receives his beliefs through his emotions. In the contact with truth-facts the appreciator receives his beliefs through his reason. In the former case he is so to speak suffused, while in the latter he is convinced. In the former he is paradoxically always at once at home, while in the latter he has to surmount the feeling of strangeness. Where there is sufficient recognition, art is everyone's home; but we sometimes have to learn how to adjust to the hard facts of actuality.

A more graphic illustration can be elicited from works of art themselves by means of a comparison of different types. Artistic inference moves from the actual to the possible in terms of value-fact, in contrast with scientific inference which moves from the actual to the possible in terms of truth-fact. The former seeks the symbolically singular while the latter seeks the factually universal. But artistic possibility resembles scientific possibility in no way which permits of an extended comparison. For example, *Hamlet* is symbolically true; the events it recites could have happened. But *Alice in Wonderland* is also symbolically true even though the events it recites could not have happened. If we then can discover what these two types have in common we may be close to the essence of the matter.

What the world of *Hamlet* and that of *Alice in Wonderland* have in common is an identical availability for emotional occupancy. The point is that as accounts of reality they are equal in preciseness of description, for they are describing axiological unities whose parts are value-facts. No matter that *Hamlet* could have happened and that *Alice in Wonderland* could not have happened. Accept the axioms equally and they make equal sense, and this is not controverted by the vast difference between them with respect to their departure from ordinary conceptions of actuality. Thus the truth-value of works of art refers directly to value-facts, and the availability of works of art relies exclusively upon this reference. Art can be no more generic than its truth-value allows.

V

We have reached the stage in the argument at which it is possible to claim that we have shown art to have truth-value, and this in two senses. It has the truth-value of coherence when it has a unity as represented by a single value. It has the truth-value of correspondence when the facts chosen for the correspondence are the axiological aspects of facts rather than the logical aspects. A number of points remain to be cleared up. Where there is truth-value there must be the possibility of false-value, and this both in the case of coherence and in that of correspondence. The false-value of works of art has yet to be shown. Yet to be shown also is how what I have argued to be true of literary works of art and illustrated by the use of the *Hamlet* propositions can be argued also for non-literary works of art.

The false-value of works of art in the case of coherence occurs in two separate ways. In linear systems it is apparent when there is a lack of unity resulting from inconsistency. A novel in which the protagonist was described in chapter one as having a wooden leg but in which he did not limp in later chapters would be inconsistent and would therefore lead to false-value. The false-value of works of art is apparent in circular systems in the superfluity of parts. Rococo art in which the parts are not parts of the whole but lesser wholes in themselves are good examples: unintegrated decoration and embellishment, such as characterized French art in the seventeenth century.

False-value in the case of correspondence occurs when the stale and unimaginative repetition of previous art fails to make the reference of the art it repeats and hence fails to have the same amount of impact. It is a characteristic of art that fresh work is referential, but the repetition is not. The master manages to imbue his work with a suggestiveness which his imitators fail to achieve. In false art the work has retained the object to which it refers directly but has lost the value to which it should refer indirectly. It tells a story or it makes a reference, but the immense power is gone. There is nothing in it beyond what it professes, no overtones or connections. The popular novel is apt to be of this sort. It makes an immediate appeal because its immediate object is readily evident, but the fact that it has no indirect reference is more subtle and its absence only appears as a serious limitation after its initial reception is over. Also of this sort are the imitation Greek temples which turn up all over as banks and motion picture theaters.

That there can be false-values in art discloses something of the nature of artistic inference. For there is such a thing as artistic inference if it can go wrong. We have seen that both the *Hamlet* propositions and what is subsequently true for the events that take place within the play as a result have their counterpart in non-literary works of art which require time for their unfolding, notably the theme-and-variations type of musical composition which best shows the bare skeleton of its logical structure. Yet it should be clear that we are not dealing here only with the usual sort of abstract logical deduction. Works of art are never mere illustrations of logical inference. Artistic inference is less elegant than logic, perhaps, but far richer in other ways.

Artistic inference is affective. It moves from quality to quality by means of value-fact. It has an inner necessity which is provided by the presence of logic: it is remorselessly logical. Yet art deals in wholes as logic deals in parts, wholes displaying a single face in which is contained all the power of connotation its structure can support. The appearance is one of suggestion, the connections themselves being buried under a surface impression of sporadic elements; but the more disparate these are as they occur, the surer the underlying continuum. Art, then, has a truth-value which is peculiar to it just as value is peculiar to the world though perfectly general within it.

And now perhaps we are in a position to say what that truth is. From the point of view of its truth-value, art provides the kind of immediate judgment which is made available otherwise only through the selective action of time. With time the values tend to reassert themselves in the world. This may be the result not of any esoteric property but merely of the repetition which is possible with a certain amount of duration. Time allows things to repeat themselves under the corrosive effects which separate the timely from the timeless: through time we learn what is independent of time. Art is a shorthand summary version of many generations of the disclosures of experience, accomplished all at once and presented in its entirety as a matter of conclusions, an efficient version shorn of all the impedimenta of reasons and arguments, all by itself in the morning, the universe of value symbolized in a single dazzling object with all of the power of radiation we should expect such a compression to contain.

TEN

What Is the Work of Art About?

Almost everyone, however unaccustomed to the experience of a work of art, has responded to it at some time, whether in a theater or an art gallery, or by reading a book. But few have understood what was involved. We often proceed on the assumption that because we know that a thing functions and therefore find ourselves in the position of being able to use it, we also understand *what* it is, when this is very far from being the case. We know that aspirin reduces an ordinary headache but we do not know precisely how. The knowledge of how a thing works is more readily within our grasp than the knowledge of what it is in itself; that usually remains a mystery. Art has been around a long time, of course. We know that it intensifies experience, enriches life and exercises the emotions in a positive way; yet not many have comprehended the process by which such desirable effects are achieved.

Art cannot be properly explained by talking about the artist, even though without him it would not exist. For the artist is not a part of the work of art, and often he is no longer even in the same framework that produced it. People change with time; they develop other interests and outlooks; whereas the work of art remains whatever it was at the time it was made. And so the artist's intentions, his feelings and plans, recede from the work of art as it moves away from him in time. Even though he had been responsible for its existence in the first place, it must now lead a life of its own. It is this art object, conceived as an independent entity existing in the world, about which I wish here to inquire.

Of what does the work of art consist? It may be defined as a material body which has been altered deliberately in order to feature its beauty. The beauty itself is the quality which emerges from the perfect fitting of parts in a whole. Due to the connotations of the term "beauty" the artist prefers to think of himself as in search of truth. But he does not mean the kind of truth the philosopher or the scientist seeks; he means the truth of value, which is, in one of its aspects, beauty.

Works of art are material objects which have been altered through human agency in order to feature that special property which all material things have in some measure. The arts, then, consist in one set of facts about the world expressed in a set of things which have been made by a class of gifted men who are equipped to elicit the special property.

It becomes clear what the artist's task is. We can think of it in terms of the material production of beauty. The quality of beauty itself is as intense as anything passive can be. It is

163

not an active force but it may have the *effect* of a force; it may be disturbing to that degree. The perfect fitting of parts in the whole is what Plato called harmony, and the quality in question has been described as giving off a peculiar radiance, so it would not be too limiting to describe a work of art as a material object characterized by the radiance of harmony.

In the effort to clarify what a work of art is about it might be helpful to have recourse to a distinction made by the great German logician Gottlob Frege. Propositions, he said, have sense (*Sinn*) and reference (*Bedeutung*). Both have objects. The sense of a proposition is its meaning; the reference is to objects. The sense would have to be logical for we are talking about *meaning*. The reference could be logical or material. But the meaning of a proposition is independent of the proposition, else it could not be what the proposition means. What a term means has nothing to do with truth or falsity; it means whatever it means. There are no false meanings any more than there are true ones.

The situation in regard to reference, however, is quite different. The reference could be logical or it could be material. The reference of "2" in "2 + 2 = 4" obviously refers to a logical object. The reference of "chair" in "My chair has a design on the back" is to a material object. All propositions in logic and mathematics have references to logical objects, all propositions in empirical science have references to material objects. However, it should be noted that the reference to material objects is indirect; the direct reference is always logical. Signs, like propositions, have both sense and reference. Indeed all the references of signs, except proper names, are to universal classes directly and to members of the classes only indirectly.

When and only when the sign is a proper name, is the reference to a material object directly.

It should be remembered at this point that a work of art is a symbol, and a symbol is a sign whose leading edge is a quality.

Before we apply the distinction between sense and reference to the work of art, one more distinction must be raised. This is the one between a true proposition and a false one. We have been discussing only true propositions, but what about the sense and the reference of false propositions? We shall need to know more about this before taking up the question of works of art.

It happens that the false proposition can have sense but no reference. If I were to say, "The moon is made of green cheese," anyone who heard me would know exactly what I meant, because almost everyone has seen the moon, tasted cheese and encountered things which were made of other things. But since the moon is very certainly *not* made of green cheese, the sentence is false. Thus it is possible to have sense without reference but not possible to have reference without sense. If a proposition refers to something it must mean something. In the latter instance of course the sense would be general and the reference particular. If I were to say, "That is a handsome dog," pointing as I did to a particular animal we could both see, then you would immediately recognize the reference but you would perhaps not as immediately recognize that I was connecting two abstract classes in order to make the reference. But it would be necessary to do so because not all things are dogs and not all dogs are handsome.

Now let us substitute for the proposition a work of art. To what, we may ask, does the work of art refer? How does it stand with respect to sense and reference? The answer is a simple one though perhaps not so easy to grasp. For art makes ordinary sense but has a peculiar kind of reference. The sense of a work of art is its meaning, and the meaning of art can be separated from its reference. We all know and understand what *Hamlet* means even though there was no man who had been named in this way. A work of art has reference of a peculiar sort which I will undertake to discuss presently. Meanwhile I should like to concentrate on its meaning for the moment. The meaning of a work of art is a qualitative affair. It is common enough to ask in puzzlement what a particular work of art "means" and just as often and just as common to be told that such a question cannot be answered didactically. The meaning is an intense quality and qualities cannot be described easily, if indeed they can be described at all.

To express such a meaning is the whole aim of the art, and to comprehend it is the task of the appreciator. How are we to help him when his appreciation depends to some extent upon the amount of his equipment? He must be somehow in the perspective which the enjoyment of a work of art requires as its precondition. But if he is in that perspective then he knows what it "means" even though he may not himself be in a position to say just what that meaning is. To feel it may be quite enough.

Now let us get to the reference. And let us take for our illustration Gainsborough's "Portrait of Lady Hamilton." Just what is the reference of this work of art? Not Lady Hamilton, and this for two reasons: In the first place, she is long dead; and in the second she probably never looked exactly like this, not, that is, if it really is a work of art, for art does not copy actuality but instead takes off from it to express—yes, that is correct, to express—meanings. The reference of this painting is to a possible object, not to an actual object, to a Lady Hamilton who could have existed, not precisely to the one who did exist. A work of art refers to a possible set of conditions, not to an actual one, even though suggested by an actual one.

There may be a gain in understanding if we pause for a moment to compare the statements of art with those of science. The statements of art, say in literature, are qualitative meanings with reference to specific states of affairs. The statements of science, say in physics, are quantitative meanings with reference to specific states of affairs, in this case to all possible states of affairs of a certain class. Art means something specific but refers to something general, whereas science means something general but refers to something specific. It is easy to note from this contrast that the meaning and the reference of a work of art may be intimately connected, whereas in science they are more distinct. Nothing is hurt by the fact that the particulars of art are pseudo-particulars while those of science are genuine.

Both art and science are concerned with world conditions; but science is concerned with the conditions of this actual world, including its possibilities only because it has a past in which some no longer exist and a future in which they do not exist yet; while art is concerned with the conditions of possible worlds, *excluding those of this material one.* The descriptions of art never fit those of actual conditions, but the descriptions of science are aimed at doing exactly that, even though they never do it absolutely.

In the sense that art is never a description of actual conditions it can be said to be false. Indeed art does consist in sets of false propositions. Not all false propositions are works of art, of course, but all works of art are false propositions. There never was an Achilles, a Macbeth, a Raskolnikov. However, an artistic proposition does not, like a logically false proposition, imply all propositions but instead implies only those propositions which are consistent with it. A work of art is a consistent system and so has the truth of consistency even though it lacks the truth of correspondence.

What keeps the work of art from being the same as any false proposition is its consistency and its cogency. The work of art may not be a description of this material world but it is a description of a possible world. A possible world is a world made up of the elements contained in, or those suggested by, this actual material world but arranged differently. It is the only way in which men are able to make contact with possible worlds. For the arrangement of things in this world is not the only possible arrangement. It is the only *actual* arrangement and therefore performs the role of touchstone for human life. But the imagination has the power to suggest how things could be other than how they are, and therefore provides an instrument for getting in touch with possible worlds.

The logic of art is not quite the simple affair that my remarks thus far would seem to say it is. Not only is art made up of a consistent set of contrary-to-fact conditionals, but I would insist that any consistent set of contrary-to-fact conditionals is a work of art. I must remind my reader at this point that not all works of art are great art. To substantiate that claim something else has to be added to the mixture, namely, a significance, which I shall try to describe when I discuss the role of the imagination at the end of this study. In the meanwhile it will be best to concentrate on the logical aspects.

Contrary-to-fact conditionals, or propositions in the subjunctive mood, describe states of affairs which may never come to pass. They may be inconsistent with the conditions of existence but they are not internally inconsistent, which is all that we need to know to understand them as works of art. Art does exist, of course, but it is the opportunity taken in existence to describe states of affairs which do not exist but which are suggested by certain states of affairs which do. We live in one world but we can conceive of others, and such conceptions often illuminate the world in which we live in a surprising manner which both intensifies and delights. There is by definition no monotony to variety, no similarity to differences.

From this we can see something of the range and the power which art provides. It widens the experience considerably by putting us into contact with some of the possible worlds. Possible worlds are contrary-to-fact if by "fact" we refer to true statements about this actual material world, but they have their own logic and their own interior sets of conditions, their own "facts." A work of art may be described in this connection as a qualitative symbol of some other alternative world.

It should be remembered at this point that a work of art is a symbol, and a symbol is a sign whose leading edge is a quality. The quality has a radiance which strikes the feelings of the appreciator forcibly. A great work of art is one which is capable of making each of us feel that it is somehow his own private possession. Yet no one owns a Bach fugue, a Homeric epic, a Shakespearean play. Its sense of universal privacy is the property of the culture and of anyone capable of sharing its privileges.

Now if we revert to the distinction introduced earlier between sense and reference we can make a new use of it and so illuminate the answer to the question of what the work of art is about. The sense of a work of art is its meaning. The possible world which it describes is its reference. And they are not the same. The meaning is the quality of the referent. The meaning of a work of art is more immediate: a story, a portrait, a musical pattern sets it forth. The meaning may be grasped in a single impression, as in a lyric poem or a statue, or it may take time for its unfolding, as in a novel, a play, or a symphony. In either case, however, we are confronted with its meaning. To produce a work of art is to put something out in the world which was not there before except as a possibility. Once it is there it makes a claim of its own. It has a stubborn existence with which the artist, like everyone else, must reckon. It becomes a fact, as indestructible as any other. Art, in other words, has its own rules, its own terms and conditions, which it imposes just as surely as any other material object does.

Finally, let us talk about the ultimate reference of the work of art. The faculty of imagination is the capacity to understand the extent to which disparate parts of the world are woven together. The work of art refers indirectly by communicating directly, and what it refers to is the value of the unity of the world as concentrated in the quality of its symbolic counterpart. From a given perspective in which the whole involvement of a work of art becomes available, its occupant is made to feel that he belongs, as himself a part, to the largest unity.

PART FOUR
Criticism

ELEVEN

The Criticism of Art

In this chapter I propose to examine the criticism of art. I shall do so under the following topics. (I) What are the problems of art criticism? (II) What is the equipment of the critic? (III) What is his function? (IV) How does he perform it?

I

The central problem in the criticism of art is the evaluation of new works of art and the reevaluation of the classics. Mr. Huntington Cairns in his Introduction to *Lectures in Criticism* [1] has stated the tasks in such excellent terms that his words must be considered by anyone who would enter upon an examination of criticism. The critic, Mr. Cairns says, seeks to judge and explain. The aim of this chapter is

[1] New York 1949, Pantheon Books.

to encompass the theory of criticism in such a way that a prospective theorist would know with what he was confronted.

One question for the critic always is, of what solid worth is the product which the imagination of the artist has brought into the world? The eruption into existence of a vigorous art must inevitably have a cruel effect. It tears at our sensibilities and challenges our established evaluations in a way most likely (if often least calculated) to occasion resentment. Something, someone, is needed to cushion the shock. Explanations are loudly demanded and softly provided, and gradually after the uproar the situation settles down to accommodate the new and startling insight. It is repulsive, it is not valuable, it is impressive, it is overwhelming, it is customary, it is a bit old-fashioned—this is the rise and fall and these are the stages of acceptance which follow when the presence of novelty in a work of art constitutes a challenge.

But there are other cases where power is the chief factor, where the novelty consists in the force rather than the forms; a Bach for example or a Shakespeare. Here the critic has an easier task in one way and a more difficult one in another; easier because he is not called upon to explain away an assault upon taste, more difficult because the superiority of the quality is subtler and harder to point out.

The art critic stands midway between theory and practice. The theory is the philosophy of art, the practice is the work of art itself. The professional theoretical field of the critic of art is of course aesthetics and his practice applied aesthetics. He is confronted with the work of art when the artist exhibits it to the public in an art gallery, at a concert, on a stage, in an edifice, or by means of a book. But on it he

must bring bearings taken from his knowledge of philosophy. The highest criticism and the soundest, Sir Joshua
Reynolds has said, is that which "refers to the eternal and
immutable nature of things."[2] Similarly, Gombrich argues
that when the Chinese artist conjures up mountains, trees
and flowers, "he does so to record and evoke a mood which
is deeply rooted in Chinese ideas about the nature of the
universe."[3] Art has its own form of communication. It is
constructed with the aim of communicating qualities,
qualities of a specific sort: aesthetic qualities. The work of
art appeals first and directly to the emotions of the appreciator. But with what? The critic has the task of eliciting
from art just those reactions which have gone into it, and
aesthetics provides the reasons.

Various theories of aesthetics exist, but they have in
common that they are equally abstract, suspended somewhere between the more general theory of an unqualified
ontology on the one side and particular works of art on the
other. If aesthetics is the theory of a particular region of ontology, namely, that region defined by the qualities which
emerge from the bonds between parts, and if the beautiful is
the quality of internal relations, then art is the disclosure of
beauty in a particular material object, and the beautiful the
quality of its internal relations. Thus the work of the artist
is at the most basic end of the aesthetic scale, while that of
the philosopher of art is at the other. Between them is the
art critic who must know what it is like to be an artist, and
be able also to put himself in the position of the philoso-

---

[2] *Discourses on Art,* Discourse 13.
[3] E. H. Gombrich, *Art and Illusion* (New York 1960, Pantheon),
p. 150.

pher. He is the middleman who interprets works of art in terms of aesthetic theory.

Such a task may seem simple yet it is not so unless the critic solves the problem of goodness of fit when selecting the aesthetic theory with which he intends to confront a particular contribution to art. Should he interpret Nadelman's sculpture by means of Aristotle's theory of art as the imitation of the ideal? Or should he condemn Andrew Wyeth for the very fact that his paintings fit Plato's theory of art as the imitation of an imitation? Is Rembrandt to be preferred to Velasquez because, while both are able to capture on canvas that sublimity to which Longinus refers, Rembrandt is able to do it for the commonplace, for a side of raw beef hanging in a butcher shop?

If the art critic stands between aesthetics and the work of art, the position of the artist is a bit more empirical, for his position lies between the observable world and aesthetics. We do have the records in some instances of the artist's preoccupation with philosophy: witness Dostoyevsky's concern with Hegel, Huysmans's with Schopenhauer, and Proust's with Leibniz and Bergson. The achievement of the artist can be enriched and deepened if first he has steeped himself in philosophy, and the critic's equipment is sharpened if he has troubled to prepare himself with a knowledge of aesthetics.

It is an able critic indeed who can employ a systematic aesthetics to illuminate the meaning of a work of art without allowing that system to constrict his efforts so firmly that the whole result becomes didactic and bears no relation to the quality of the art itself. There is the danger of immolation through an excess of order, just as there is the corresponding danger of random impressionism which results from having no order at all. One can invoke an aesthetic order through a contemplation of the work of art itself and yet leave the appreciator to remain so much without it that his participation wanders off in a vague blurring of the outlines and results finally in a neglect of the art itself. The selection of an aesthetics for use in criticism is a gamble whose results may be disastrous as well as fortuitous, yet the gamble must be taken.

Thus far we have been talking about the critic's role of confronting the problems presented by the new work of art. But in addition to the evaluation of new works of art, there is also the task of the reevaluation of the classics. This second task is an equally sophisticated one, calling on all the cultural powers of the art critic. It was more imperative perhaps to direct attention to the plays of Shakespeare because of their artistic success than it was to divert attention from the plays of Seneca because of their artistic failure, but both were necessary.

Seneca was a Roman, Shakespeare an Englishman, but no matter. As art extends beyond cultural boundaries so must the critic's knowledge and judgment. For the critic, like the scientist or the philosopher, looks beyond the narrow boundaries of his own culture in order to understand that culture itself. He must be able to see it in some sort of perspective in which it is revealed as a whole in order to bring the gift of breadth to its parts. Completeness as well as consistency is required to give perspective to any element of culture which is as deeply imbedded in it as an established work of art is sure to be.

It is in the light of the accepted and approved values of his age—and as much in the overt and explicit theories of value as in the more covert and implicit values which are thrown up around him—that the philosophically-equipped critic will seek what that perspective can tell him about works of art whose position of eminence, or lack of it, was previously long established. Consider for example some of the recent criticism of *Hamlet* made on the basis of contemporary theories. We may take one from psychology, more specifically from psychoanalysis, and another from politics, as illustrated by dialectical materialism. For the psychoanalysts Hamlet's problem "can be solved by reference to the Oedipus complex"[4]: he was in love with his mother and consequently jealous of his uncle. For the Marxists, Hamlet was crushed by the economic class struggle. He was "caught between the corruption in the court, the vulgarity of the growing bourgeoisie, and the masses in whom he has no belief."[5] The critic has the specific assignment of examining these theories.

II

What faculties are available for the criticism of art? This question is easy enough to answer when we consider the limited number which are available for any human disposal. The critic, like everyone else, can call on (1) thought, (2) feeling and (3) action. Let us consider how each of them in turn has been utilized by him in the process of art criticism.

1. All reasoning concerning the value of a work of art has to begin with principles, presumably with those of a deductive system. An aesthetic system would be the most appro-

[4] Sigmund Freud, *An Outline of Psychoanalysis.* Trans. James Strachey. New York 1949. W. W. Norton. P. 96.
[5] A. A. Smirnov, *Shakespeare: A Marxist Interpretation.* New York 1936. Critic's Group. P. 66.

priate, and in most cases aesthetics is a special application of a metaphysics. In short, this method would consist in applying a metaphysics to an aesthetics and then an aesthetics to a particular work of art. Two deductive steps are thus involved, and they call on the art critic for a very considerable knowledge of philosophy.

2. The utilization of feeling in art criticism occurs as the intuition of its value. The art critic therefore must be in possession of superior sensitivity; he must be so constructed that his sensibilities are above the average and he must have sharpened them on habitual application of the evaluation of particular works of art. Baudelaire often employed his own immense sensitivity in the appreciation of painting, and it was this perhaps that enabled him to recognize the power of Delacroix. Such perceptiveness no doubt presupposes delicate equipment and long practice. It would require on the part of the art critic that he himself function as a recording instrument capable of making the proper qualitative judgments.

3. The role of action in art criticism could come about because the art critic himself was a practicing artist. There is no substitute for immersion in the activity engendered by a field if the understanding of it is to be achieved. The practice of an art takes one inside that art to its very essence, and so could lead to accurate professional judgments. Only an artist is in the last analysis capable of understanding what almost insuperable problems have been solved and what gains achieved by another artist. The recognition of the greatness of Matthew Smith in England was certainly initiated by the holding of a one-man show of those of his paintings which were in the possession of Jacob Epstein.

Each of the three faculties however has its limitations as a sufficient equipment for the art critic, and we may next look at some of the reasons why no one of them by itself is enough.

1. First, as to the limitations of thought. The rigid deductive systems which characterize metaphysics and aesthetics at this stage of their development lead to a deadly accuracy when the aim is good, but to a radical absurdity when it is not. All deductive systems are linear, and when a linear system goes wrong because its axioms are insufficient or because there have been errors in the reasoning it goes very wrong. It is not only the inconsistency of the rationalist or the inadequacy of his axioms which could be at fault but also the incompleteness of his system. What is not included in a system which is relevant can destroy the value of the system. Now since most deductive systems have been checked and rechecked for consistency, this is not the property which is usually at fault. Rather it is the completeness. Bergson's chief merit is to have shown that the changing world is richer than any of our limited schemes. No one has yet been able to encompass the drama of Shakespeare in a philosophy. The excluded elements in a deductive system rather than those which are contained in it often succeed in faulting the system. Thus the attempt to evaluate works of art by measuring them against didactic theories of what a work of art should be are apt to fail of their purpose.

2. Next we have to consider the limitations of feelings. The intuitions are at best an uncertain guide to the truth. It is easy to claim superiority in this case but quite another thing to substantiate the claim. And are there valid grounds on which the claim could be based? For what reason should we concede that the sensibilities of the art critic are superior

to those of the artist or his public and more to be accepted as authentic than those of the technician or the appreciator? The only possible evidence that could be adduced for the authority of intuition would be the success of the judgments made on the basis of it. How are we to know when the correct evaluation of a work of art has been made? One can only assume that a sufficient number of judgments (more than can be gathered in any single generation or in any one period when there are other values) tends to approach the truth if not to equal it. But if this is the case, then the intuition holds no superior place over the other faculties. One serves as well as another in a statistical estimate where what counts is the number of informed and concerned judgments rather than the special qualifications of any subgroup of them.

3. Finally, we need to look at the limitations of action. There is one supreme difficulty in placing the practicing artist in the role of art critic. He is neither impartial nor detached. The practicing critic injects himself into the practical situation, we have noted, by making judgments which materially affect the immediate fate of the artist. His reception depends upon favorable criticism and his rejection may be the result of it. The weight of criticism, then, is a heavy one. Who in such a case is entitled to feel qualified to accept the responsibility for the effects of a decision which subsequent generations may upset so radically? To take no action when one is a professional is of course to take action of a sort, but this does not rob the activity of its perils.

What conclusions are we to draw from our analysis of the critic's use of his capacity for thought, feeling and action? That these separately are inadequate as equipment for the critic, or perhaps that art criticism itself is impossible?

CRITICISM

There is one last alternative which has not yet been considered. Can all three faculties, all of those of which the critic is possessed, be organized together in such a way that they constitute a sufficient force to generate a proper criticism?

Although individual man acts as a whole it is not always the whole man who is acting. For the art critic has his own method, his own technique and his own special skills and talents. He can imaginatively lead the appreciator with him into a work of art by means of myth or analogy or some appropriate figure. In this form of explanation the critic becomes a minor artist whose accomplishment serves to make some major art available. The extreme of this sort of wholesale approval is the invention of another and lesser work of art, so that the critic has himself become an artist and his criticism art. Witness Virgil's redoing of Homer and Shaw's version of Chekhov.

There is no doubt of the items which the critic must be able to count among his equipment. He must know and feel his way inside some particular aesthetic theory, so that he does not look directly at it and indeed may not any longer be aware of it yet is able to see works of art from it. He must be familiar with that special art which as his life work he has chosen to interpret. But these are nothing without that element of origination which enables him to see the relevancy of the connection between the theory he espouses and the art he judges and so to apply the former to the latter with accuracy and disclosure.

The leading edge of his judgment will have to be powered by an incisive insight into the object of the artist's aim. Such an aim does not need to have been conscious or deliberate but it does have to have an object in view, and the critic has to be able to elicit it. And he has to be able to fit the evaluation to the value without superfluous calculation. Now all decisions which prove to have any stable worth are made through feeling rather than from reasons. That is, they are made on *immediate* feeling rather than from *direct* reasons. It happens, however, that the feelings of a rational man are more rational than those of an irrational man, always provided of course that the feelings are retained along with the reason. The aesthetic theory which the critic employs in order to decide about the value (or disvalue) of a particular work of art must be in the background rather than the foreground, it must remain unconscious rather than become conscious, if it is to serve him best.

All works of art have the strong feature in common that they are works of art, but they also have many important differences. In the domain of aesthetics diverse aesthetic theories may be regarded as opposed, and bitter battles of discourse have been fought to prove one right, another wrong. Aesthetics is a particular region of ontology and ontologies are mood music, designed to fit special areas of being. Aesthetic theories may be safely regarded in the same way. One school of art is best explained by one art theory, and another by another. Martial music is not the same as love music, and if a single aesthetic theory be employed to illuminate them both, something is likely to be obscured instead. For different works of art may say different things about existence and not be in conflict or false, but the two together could still be incompatible, as qualities are in Leibniz' theory of compossibles.

And so two kinds of fitting are called for by the art critic. He must first be able to identify a work of art by means of his knowledge of art history, and then he must be able to illuminate it by his ability to select just that aesthetic theory which will satisfy goodness of fit.

A few examples of what I have been saying might make these points clearer. Augustine's theory of art could be used best to explain Picasso's "Guernica." The expression of repulsion at fascist cruelty is borne out by objects which relative to others lack symmetry. Ugliness is in Augustine's view comparative deformity. It illuminates the harmony of cosmic beauty. The contrast is dramatic and emotionally illustrative. In the still framework of the horror of war it is possible to see the peaceful fitness of things.

That measured art which sees the ideal in the commonplace, as Cézanne did in his painting of the house at the turn of the road, "La maison du pendu," was forecast by Francis Hutcheson two hundred years earlier, for he understood that the imitation of an object could be beautiful when the original was entirely devoid of it. It is the qualities of the human intellect which match the harmony in the object, Price said in support of Hutcheson's view. Cézanne showed that the use of the intellect in no wise detracts from the effect of the emotions, an element in his painting which his imitators have missed.

The skill of the critic consists chiefly in his ability to recognize in what is new and valuable a continuance of tradition. See for example the homage accorded Hans Hofmann by Brian O'Doherty in *The New York Times* for September 11, 1963, on the occasion of that painter's retrospective exhibition at the Museum of Modern Art. Mr. O'Doherty in characteristic fashion not only acclaims the established position achieved by the aging avant-garde painter but explains why he deserves it. Hofmann, in O'Doherty's view, "outlasted most of the abstract expressionists he helped to father" by "holding that movement's violence within a rugged, semi-classical discipline."

The critic both welcomes and celebrates great art but also accedes to the reinterpretation of tradition which its arrival constitutes. For every novel work of art not only grants us a fresh additional element with which to deepen and widen our experience and hence our very life but also reconstitutes the past in assimilable form. It furnishes us with a perspective which renders the best of the past more intelligible because it is more in the terms with which we are destined to become familiar.

Good taste in judging art presupposes a sense of proportion; but this the critic may have without also having that discernment of the form of a work of art on which his sense of proportion may be exercised. The proportions vary with the novelty and with the magnitude of the art, and its very achievement may blind him to its proportions; for the shapes of power are crude more often than not. How wrong it is yet how common to mistake refinement for achievement, delicate sensibilities for overwhelming **force**! Only with proper lapse of time and the due process of apotheosis can a dead genius be permitted the vulgarities in which he may have indulged. Shakespeare's bawdy has been reinstituted, with even a volume by that title devoted to it, little more than a century after Dr. Thomas Bowdler published his expurgated "family" edition. Yet it is that same mistake which convinces the art critic that he and the work of art share a high value from which the artist with his disarrayed clothing, his dirty studio and his unconventional life are fortunately excluded.

The opposite viewpoint also exists of course and its effects are equally undesirable. The vogue for the latest wrinkle which makes the critic reluctantly go along, also insures bad artists a good living and their work a prominent place, at least for a while. For contemporary values have a way of disappearing when they are no longer contemporary, as when something new is mistaken for something valuable simply because its very high contemporaneity was assumed to be the value which would last. What happened to neoclassicism, to David and the French rococo of the early eighteenth century, to twentieth century surrealism? A history of bad art which had once been the vogue is seriously needed for its illustrative value. Fashions may occur as much in the recognition of art as in the proclamations of the art critic, and he may as easily be led as lead. The procession is a dizzy one, and it is sometimes hard to tell who is influencing whom.

We know this much however: that the critic accepts the work of art on its own terms and only has to determine whether or not they have been met. The critical apparatus must be in the possession of the critic, though its use may be postponed until the measure of the work under consideration can be taken. He may have the ability to shift from his feelings and the evaluations they engender to his reasons and the judgments they dictate. He must be as much at home in one system as in another, and in possession of that ability to draw the two together in such a way that the solid properties of the work of art stand out, as it were, under his selection of features almost as much as they did at the hands of the artist.

III

Presumably every new work of art constitutes a fresh challenge to the critic. Who has ever previously encountered

anything which would have led him to expect the sculpture
of Lipchitz or of Moore, the paintings of Pollock or of
Rothko, the music of Cage or of Stockhausen? Despite his
breadth of experience, in such cases the critic is nevertheless
obliged to begin each time from the beginning and to make
an inductive formal analysis. He must in short construe its
value as the instance of a general principle of value, of
which he has (by definition) only one instance before him.
He has had many experiences of fresh works of art but no
experiences of *this* one.

It should be possible first to deduce from aesthetic theory
the principles of art criticism, and then to apply those principles to the criticism of concrete works of art. The first step
is the deduction of a less general theory from a more general
theory, and the second the deduction of a particular theory
from a general theory. For the evaluation of a concrete work
of art must remain a theory so long as we have no way of
demonstrating with certainty its correctness.

But then it must be possible to go equally far in the opposite direction, that is to say, from the new work of art to
the aesthetic theory. The original work of art if it has power
is, like all novel things, endowed with the dazzling freshness
that seems to have little of the old principles about it. In the
morning the world seems new and without rules, and a
great contribution to art is for the world another morning.
The critic has the supreme task and great privilege of having to tone down the brightness sufficiently to make it seem
tame enough for the casual man to approach.

It is not in mere enjoyment but in the deepening of all
subsequent experience that the value of a work of art
resides, and this distinction can hardly be ignored by the
astute critic who wishes to help the uninstructed to see what

he sees. It is the task of the critic to show the spectator how to permit the work of art to penetrate to deep layers of his psychological being carrying pleasure with it, and how such an experience will enable that same individual to appreciate the depths of ordinary life. For just as street music makes a ballet of business traffic so other arts intensify experience with other varieties of conventional existence in a way which shows that there are elements capable of saving practically anything from banality.

The critic has his negative assignments which are as necessary as they are painful: for in addition to recognizing and proclaiming artistic merit he has the duty of rejecting those works of art in which he finds it lacking or, more serious still, in which the substitution of lesser values has deceived many people into supposing that what they are experiencing is aesthetic and elevating rather than conventional and degrading. Not all imitation results in bad art, of course, though it may in art of a second order. Virgil is not to be thrown out because of the influence of Homer any more than *Carmen Jones* because of *Carmen* even though the result was not first rate in either case. It is the amateur who likes only the best.

He can do quickly and efficiently what the repetition of time does slowly and fumblingly. There is a connection between time and value though it has never been completely spelled out. The repeated exposures to an unworthy work of art serves, as that background slowly shifts and changes, to provide the instrument of erosion which consigns the work itself to that limbo of forgotten art with which the past must be littered. We carry enough with us from generation to generation; but for one Homer or Shakespeare, one Bach or Mozart, one Michelangelo or Velasquez, how many million of others there were who tried and failed and died happily because convinced by the admiration of their contemporaries of the solid success of their work?

We could well ask, if time alone will do this why do we need the critic in this capacity, when time, having the kindness to await the death of the artist, proves so much more merciful? Too many people are led astray and their sensibilities bruised in the period before the verdict of time has been rendered. We must sacrifice the bad artist to the needs of his audience, even risking as we do in the process the mistakes in recognition to which the critic is always liable. For he will save the audience from bad art, while the audience will save him from the penalties he perhaps has incurred for condemning the great art which instead he should have proclaimed.

The very existence of the art critic attests to the necessity for maintaining the position and aim of an unfocused estimate in the target area into which works of art can be projected at the discretion of the artist. The projection is always at the artist's peril, of course, yet of necessity: for he knows that eventually he must take his chances. He knew it already when first he decided to become an artist and to submit his efforts to criticism, and he was willing to do so on the ground that their claim to value and longevity as material objects in the world exceeded those of himself as a person. He intends his art not to die while knowing that he himself will. To have limitations means also to have value—there must be something which is limited. The artist is not ideal and his work is not perfect. And neither is the art critic who will make mistakes when undertaking judgments. All three, the artist, the art and the critic, must somehow come to terms not only with the achievements but also with the shortcomings of art.

The critic is alleged to have the license to bestow the certificate of gentility upon the qualitative products of power. At his assent the sharp edges of art become subtleties to be admired even when they hurt, and at his suggestion appreciators approach works of art in an attitude most likely to secure their approval. He can prepare those who come to a work of art with the proper emotional setting in which to receive it and so win some victories for art which it would otherwise lose either through seeming repellent to the unprepared or through simple lack of notice to the initiated.

IV

Let us suppose that the critic first explores the work of art on its own grounds. He looks perhaps for completeness: what does the work include? Then he looks for consistency: what did it set out to portray? Inductively, he works backward from the results to the intention: are there any incongrous elements? What did the artist set out to accomplish, what was his explicit aim? If the work of art possesses any merit at all it will have a central design. In most cases a principle of harmony can be discerned but a consistent principle of incongruity will do just as well; for there are baroque as well as classical undertakings which are acceptable.

We have said that the critic's final task after his preliminary work is done is to warn others away from bad art and to assist them in the appreciation of great art. The former is accomplished through the exposure of weaknesses and flaws in the art under examination. The latter is accomplished through the naming and explaining of the kind of reaction which is to be expected if the appreciation of a work of art is to measure up to its merits. The critic can do this last either didactically, by patiently explaining what he has found, or indirectly, by transmitting the emotional impact of the work of art into the medium of his own capacity for self-expression.

The critic is needed and needed badly, but he is an applied aesthetician who requires someone to fashion the tools of his trade before he can develop the skills to use them. In his time it is too late to develop the aesthetics appropriate to it; that must have been done previously. The critic and not the aesthetician is the man of the hour. He is if he is capable just what the art and the audience of his time deserve. And so he bestows a facility upon them and a mode of coming together which they would never have had without him.

The emotional expression of the critic's own reaction as appreciator reconstructs in another medium, that of language, one evaluation of the value of a work of art. The critic thus attempts to become the archetypal appreciator, a model for others. He can reduce to reasons what he apprehends as feeling. He can endeavor to explain didactically what he knows through his senses to be there. It often happens that when we are equipped with logic we can the more readily apprehend value. Inference helps us to see more deeply into relations, and it is the relations which carry the values.

In appraising a work of art, it is easy to affect talents, to pretend to a style, to boast of the virtues of possessing exquisite sensibilities, in ways which leave the uninstructed impressed and with no reason to suspect that the sought for (but unfounded) enthusiasm has been shifted without warrant from the effect of the work of art to the critic himself.

CRITICISM

We should remind ourselves that it is the critic's glasses we want, but in order to see through them, not to look at them. An over-zealous art critic can so easily become an end in himself, and when he does then it is the very appreciation of art that he most obscures. How many readers has Walter Pater escorted to the art of the Renaissance and how many others only to Walter Pater? It is always possible that the guide can justify himself by leading us past values more important than were to have been reached by the main road. But such accidents are rare, and it more often happens that we are led into a blind alley—one no less blind for being paved with elaborate decorations.

The great critic will express in himself the values of his age; he will want what his culture wants and reject what it rejects. But his evaluations will be more stable and less temporary than many other expressions of the culture which are of a less specialized nature. Monotony is death, and so it is the privilege of the critic that he conducts us back to that renewal of life which the work of art instigates.

An idiom begins as an insight and ends as an insult. It is a free gift to invite the spectator to share some pleasurable and enlightening experience, but it is only an affront to remind him again of what he had agreed to accept even though all of the positive values of experience have long gone out of it. Classic art permits the acknowledgment of the splendor of being, romantic art reminds us that our participation in being might become somewhat more than it is.

The impressionistic critic at his best endeavors to express in luminous language the aesthetic quality he experiences when confronted with a work of art for which he seeks appreciation in others. Through its very intensity he is able to explore its range. He can bring the studio attitude to the spectator in the museum, and to those who have not more than a postman's interest in letters he can give it something of what the familiar gossips get out of the letters. The judgment of the impressionistic critic is no ordinary judgment appropriate to common sense but the kind of blinding insight which illuminates almost unbearably when it does not go wrong; not a display of learning but an ability to recoil sensibly when the stimulation is as forceful as a successful work of art.

An ideal is suggested by those objects which fall short of it. The critic is more aware of this than are others among his contemporaries and he has the task of reminding them. For he sees not directly into nature, as the artist does, but into the artist's aims; and not into the aim of one artist only but of many, so that his nature is compounded of a thousand perspectives and he learns to recognize and to appraise with a professional eye the extent to which nature has been interpreted, selected or suborned. The critic helps us to put ourselves in the position not only of the artist but better still of the work of art itself. He enables us to acquire from the work of art that capacity for intensified experience which can be the result of our encounter with it.

Every work of art which stands out for its merit does so against the nameless background of all those countless works which have faded through justifiable neglect and been excusably forgotten, remembered only in the aggregate and as shadows sufficient to afford for success the depth of a needed dimension. If it is of value in his opinion, then how much? By this time he has got down fairly to cases. He can now drag out his file of typological studies and see if he has a card to fit. If he has one that matches too well then this is suspicious; if he has none he will have to fall back and re-group his resources, for perhaps the art which confronts him is more overpowering than he had at first supposed.

But the critic is not an official and his judgments and explanations are not final. No criticism is absolute, and each competent critic only contributes what he can to the body of criticism. Like the coral of an atoll, the pronouncements of the critics together eventually build a cohesive island of opinion concerning a work of art; and if such opinion have no more stability than a continually re-vised statistical trend, still it helps in establishing that position for the art to which by its merit it is entitled.

TWELVE

On the Metaphysics of
the Performing Arts

In this chapter I want to set forth some of the ontological properties of the performing arts. I cannot be specific about this, however, without first saying what I understand by the arts. Let me repeat some definitions.

By *beauty* I mean the radiant quality which emerges from the perfect relations of parts in a whole. More briefly, it is the quality of internal relations. The "parts" and the "whole" in this case are material things. The "radiant quality" is that quality which bears a certain effulgence; perhaps something like what Longinus meant by the sublime.

By *art* I mean the production of beauty in an artifact. An *artifact* for this purpose is a material object which has been altered through human agency. No doubt beauty exists in unaltered material objects; it exists in sunsets and mountains, in human faces and in effluviana. Yet these things are not works of art even though the distinction may be merely definitional.

I have been employing the term *material* importantly, and so perhaps a definition of it is also necessary. If substance be defined as the irrational ground of individual reaction, then matter is static substance, just as energy is dynamic substance, with the two of course permanently interchangeable.

One more definition, this one of a peculiar sort, and I am ready to define a work of art. The peculiar definition is reminiscent of something Whitehead mentioned in passing: that art consists in a set of false propositions. He was thinking primarily, of course, of the literary arts but the same description would apply *pari passu* to the other arts.

A proposition which is true to feeling may be false to fact, which is only another way of saying that feelings are often more representative of systems of ideas than are facts. It is easier to make a system of false propositions than of true ones, which is why works of art more nearly resemble false propositions. The subjunctive nature of contrary-to-fact conditionals has been recognized, but not that the relevant facts are peculiarly local. A system of ideas locally false to fact may be generally true to facts from a wider universe. Thus *Alice in Wonderland* is false to the facts represented by little girls in living rooms but true to a wider universe in which the facts are selected from human behavior generally. "The best way to explain it is to do it" does not apply to those animals which are trying to get dry after swimming in a pool of tears but may apply to all those inadequate explanations which try to get by with examples.

A *work of art* is a representation, in one or more material objects and by means of a language or other artifact, of a consistent set of false propositions whose import can be effective in impressing upon an appreciator the radiant quality which emerges from the perfection of internal relations.

Elsewhere I have dealt with the direct impact of works of art on appreciators. Here I undertake to consider the situation in which the work of a second group of artists is necessarily interpolated between the work of art and the appreciator, the interpretive artists.

By *the interpretive arts* I mean those arts which cannot be appreciated without the intermediation of the work of interpretive artists. The currently fashionable name for interpretive artists is performing artists and their arts are called the performing arts. Musical scores need to be played, choreographic directions need to be followed in the dances, dramas need to be acted. The aim of the performing artist is to put the appreciator in contact with the work of art. To do so well means for the performing artist to do it as unobtrusively as possible, to make of himself a medium of communication through which the work of art can have its greatest effect. An example of the perfection of performing art would be that occasion upon which the appreciator was made to forget that anything or anyone stood between him and the work of art, to feel and to think the art itself and not the performer.

In terms of the definitions given above we might now look at the performing arts. The performing artist or—because there is usually more than one employed in any single act of interpretation or presentation—performing artists may be thought of as the moving parts of the artifact which was expressly designed to irradiate the appreciator with its effulgence in its capacity as a work of art. In this way the performing artists render concrete the ideal world of the ought-to-be which is conveyed by the false propositions.

The "truth" of false propositions can be stated only as ideals, only by means of the "ought." They are given over to the performing artist to render actual as best he may. Ontologically, his task is not to put something else into the world but merely to emphasize and underline the work of art by making it concrete through vividity. Here is the play *Hamlet,* the best actor says; here is the ballet *Les Sylphides,* the best dancer conveys; and here happily is nothing else. The illusion of art, that in this way we are encountering things-as-they-ought-to-be as though they were things-as-they-are without intermediation, that is the ambition and the effort. It requires of the performing artist a complete submergence of himself in the particular work of art he is endeavoring to perform; and this is possible only to artists of the greatest dedication. The performing artist, as it were, presents himself to the work of art and asks to be used in its service. He subordinates his personality and submits his very being to whatever transformation the work of art requires.

In the uncut *Hamlet* as performed by Maurice Evans we have had an example of the performing art at its best. The lines assigned to Hamlet by Shakespeare in the play are spoken by Evans as though he had just thought of them in his capacity of thinking as Hamlet would have thought in that same situation. The result is a fresh reading that discloses meanings in the speeches themselves that had not been so well disclosed formerly. There are other good examples, such as Rubinstein performing Chopin.

In the best of the performing artists this requisite

humility, as it leads to submergence in the work of art, is always present and occurs naturally. The work of art is another world into which the performing artist must enter, bringing with him nothing that will not aid him in dedicating his voice, his movements, and his talents generally to exposition and to exposition alone. He adapts himself to the novel conditions imposed by the work of art and asks nothing for himself. He is its extension, its expression, and he is nothing more.

The performing artist is not an originative artist but one whose sensibilities exceed his capacity for initiation. He is capable of the joy of feeling the work of art as it passes through him, and he hands it on to the appreciator without any addition. He is an instrument upon which the art plays; he is the medium it employs, the added force it requires. He makes its life possible, and this in the way it intends. For the play on the written page is not a play: it was not intended merely to be read; and the musical score is not music as it rests upon the paper in a series of black dots between ruled lines: these were intended only as more or less precise directions for producing music. The performing arts are time arts, and require sequential activities for their unfolding. Also they are abstract and need filling in for their concretion. They are laid down along a time-line in a way that most of the other arts, with the exception of narrative literature, are not.

The best preparation for the full enjoyment of any performing art is a thorough acquaintance with the work of art before it is performed. The reading of a play or of a musical score will prepare the appreciator to measure the degree of interpretation which is being imposed upon him by the performing artist. The less interpretation the better. Familiarity with the original art even in its abstract form will protect the appreciator against fraudulent presentation and in a more positive way enable him to intensify the understanding he has already gained by folding into it the full import of what he sees and hears in the performance. It will be the work of art *as presented* on the stage or in the concert hall rather than the work of art *consisting in* what is presented on the stage or in the concert hall.

Oftentimes it is possible to update a work of art by deliberately giving it an interpretation which could not have been the one intended, but this sort of interpretation while often capable of revitalizing a dead work of art can also destroy it and surely does make of it something else. It runs the risk of cheapening the original, and achieves a false sense of vigor by adding activity and even a sort of violence to the original which it never contained. In performing a work of art, loud noise is not always a sure sign of vitality and exaggerated gestures do not always convey meaning.

Perhaps the most familiar example of the work of art degraded by its performance is in the translation from one medium to the other, a stage play or a motion picture of *The Brothers Karamazov,* for instance (both have been done), or a musical comedy made out of a serious play. A thoughtful reader may be asked to become a thoughtless auditor. The *Drei Groschen Oper* lost much of its charm while gaining in its musical appeal from the English original of *The Beggar's Opera.*

There are many ways unfortunately in which the necessity for interpretation through performance can be corrupted. I shall mention only two of the most familiar.

The first of these is when a weak work of art requires supplementation by the performing artist. The average stage play in any period is of this type. Great playwrights are perhaps less common than great novelists or great composers. And every play requires to be staged by many performing artists. As plays are currently written, the words are there but most of the action or "business," as it is called, is left to the invention of the director and the discretion of the cast. Hence much improvisation is called for, and who is to say when it is in the best interest of the original?

The attempt on the part of the actors to supply genuine deficiencies in the play makes of the performing artists in this case something more prominent than the play itself. The effect on the actors is deplorable. They lose all respect for the literary values, and look on theater pieces as mere vehicles for their virtuosity. The corrupting effect of the featured performers drops the quality and tone of the ensemble. Those plays offering the largest deficiencies which have to be made up by actors come to be regarded by those actors as the greatest plays. As a consequence the actors do not submerge themselves in the play but the play in the actors. All but the most discriminating members of the audience (who are always a minority) are inclined to go along with the result because they have no reason to know better.

That is why, perhaps, the greatest performances are achieved in those repertory companies in which a respect for the play as such is drilled into the actors. Notable examples are the Moscow Repertory Theatre and the Abbey Theatre of Dublin. The actors in both those companies were taught to believe that their best performances could only come from considering themselves as vehicles for the play and not the reverse. The play was to be played *through* them and not *for* them. But these are not usual cases, and they are not imitated as often as they are betrayed.

When the play is a strong work of art, then the betrayal is at its worst if the actor presumes to behave in his role as though it had been created solely in order to give him the opportunity to perform. For then the emotional meaning of the work of art becomes obscured, baffled, and, more often than not, altered into something less than it could have been. The star system seems at times almost to have been devised with this variety of corruption in view. The essence of tragedy is the victory of the vanquished, not the success of the leading man or woman. There is something definitely wrong with the performing arts when the death of Cyrano is the life blood of the matinee idol.

This brings me logically to the second way in which the necessity for interpretation through performance can be corrupted. When the ambitious—and talented—performing artist puts himself first and everything else, including the art, second, then there is a definite effect, often even a powerful one, but it is always something different and usually far less than what was contained in the work of art. Virtuosity can be immensely misleading. It emphasizes, over against the work of art interpreted, the way in which an interpretation is made.

We find our most familiar examples in music, and the place where this mistake is most often made in the United States. The solo violinist, pianist, or singer is apt to shift the attention of the audience away from the music and toward its interpretation.

The following dialogue is a true report and far from untypical.

LADY: Did you hear Menuhin last night?

CRITIC: No, what did he play?

LADY: He played magnificently.

CRITIC: I don't doubt that; but what—

LADY: There have been few concerts more divine.

CRITIC: Do you recall perhaps who wrote the music?

LADY: (impatient now with what she considered irrelevancies): O, I think it was something or other by Mozart but I am not sure. But what a magnificent performance!

This sort of response reaches its apogee with the symphony orchestra. The admiration—no, more: the adoration—accorded the conductor sometimes reaches the intensity of a religious cult. There exists a long-play orthophonic recording of music for the symphony orchestra conducted by Bruno Walter entitled *The Sound of Genius,* and this for a man who, in this connection at least, makes no sound. All of the sounds were made by members of the orchestra and the genius in question was Brahms. Walter is an able conductor, no doubt of that; but many of the members of his audience are completely unmindful not only of what this means but also of what it does *not* mean. It means that he trained the orchestra, and it means that he keeps time for them and by his presence reminds them of their training. It means that he has taught them his interpretation. But it does *not* mean that he wrote the music, or that he is responsible for it in any way. It does *not* mean that he is an originative genius of the order of a Beethoven or a Bach. Such geniuses are rare, far more rare than excellent conductors. There exists at the present time, according to a consensus of expert opinion, a number of conductors who are able to do justice to the music of the giants, but there is not one such giant produced in every century.

It seems plain enough on all counts that the performing

arts are adjunctive and supplementary. They have their place and it is a necessary one but it is not central. They exist in order to help the original arts to come alive. They breathe vitality into what would otherwise be an abstract script. But they are not themselves original except in a minor and secondary way. This is not to disparage them nor to derogate in any way the legitimacy of their role. It is no criticism to say of something secondary that it is secondary. At such lofty heights success does not mean trying to be first and failing but trying to be second and succeeding. Interpretation is not to be construed as defective origination but rather as brilliant supplementation.

The chief error behind the corruptions to which the performing artist is prone all follow from his tendency to attach himself in feeling to the members of his audience, to the spectators and appreciators. When the performing artist has them in mind rather than the work of art and seeks a unity through emotional expression with them, then he is using the work of art merely as a medium of communication. He is thereby assigning it a secondary function while he himself assumes the primary, for obviously he does not mean to be dominated by those for whom he is performing. No doubt the work of art *is* a medium of communication but it is something very much more, and it is in terms of this something more that we treasure it from one generation to the next.

The remedy or correction of the error lies in restoring to the performing situation the centrality of the work of art. Understanding deepens enjoyment. Hence the performing artist can help the most if he aims at increasing the impact of the work of art and endeavors both to illustrate and to simplify it for the purpose of securing maximum effect.

When the performing artist attaches himself in feeling to the work of art, then his sacrifice is a calculated risk; and when he conveys to the members of his audience the total force of the work of art and not the mere accent of his interpretation, then he is fulfilling his function. He has become the means by which the work of art reaches the members of the audience for whom it was intended; and though it could not do so without his performance, he recognizes in himself that he is only a stage on the way.

In this service, however, he can feel proud, and from the intimate association with the original art to which his professional life binds him he can derive everything ennobling. His participation in art is perhaps more intense than what anyone else can claim. His association with it is more indissoluble and more prolonged than even that of the originative artist who was responsible for it; for while the originative artist went on to other works of art, the performing artist remained behind and learned to live with it through the experience of successive performances. The actors in a successful repertory company spend more time with *The Cherry Orchard* than ever Chekhov did. In this way they can elicit more from it, and so do it a service which is certainly indispensable, one which more than justifies the essential and built-in humility which is the inevitable accompaniment of any secondary role.

THIRTEEN

Bad Art

The chief reason for studying bad art is because it might tell us about good art. The ugly is the positive effect of the absence of beauty, and bad art is the inadvertent production of the ugly; "inadvertent" because no one has ever set out to produce bad art, yet bad art can be and often is the side effect of an effort to produce good art.

All art aims at the beautiful though much of it misses the mark. There is of course a clear distinction between bad art and the ugly. All bad art is ugly, but the ugly is not always bad art for it may have a part to play in a work of art which is prevailingly beautiful. The ugly in fact consists in the positive effects of the failure to be beautiful, and this is not confined to art: a face may be ugly, indeed anything which exists may be, but we are concerned here chiefly with bad art.

Bad art has seldom been studied. You might go through many a history of art without seeing the topic mentioned. Often the properties of the opposite of a thing are very informative about that thing. It is the same kind of information one gets from the sally about the thinness of some of the books that might be written: *Three Hundred Years of German Humor, A History of Italian War Heroes,* or *An Irish Cookbook.* Yet one can examine volume after volume of treatises of art and aesthetics without encountering the term, bad art.

The references to bad art in the literature are few and far between. An exception is Collingwood; for him, however, bad art is "the corrupt consciousness," an "unsuccessful attempt to become conscious of a given emotion," plainly a topic in the psychology of art and not in the theory of the art object. Bad art is the result of the failure to meet aesthetic criteria, just as Morris said it is. Bad art is art though bad, while ugliness is not a negative value, for its effects may be positive. We are repelled by the ugly because there is something positive at work in it. We shall have to begin in reverse, however, and define bad art in terms of art, moving from good art to bad. Good art, incidentally, is not called good art but more simply art.

Bad art has not been considered at any length, but the ugly has. We might touch briefly on a few of the classic opinions. Aristotle was the first to mention bad art. He regarded comedy as an imitation of men worse than the average as regards the ridiculous, which was for him a species of the ugly, a view in which he was followed many centuries later by Lessing. Plutarch's concern with the ugly was chiefly devoted to the part it could play in the greater beauty of a whole work of art; he supposed that the ugly appropriately represented could be beautiful. For Plotinus the ugly either is capable of rational form and has not received it, or is incapable. Beauty is the authentic existent and "ugliness the principle contrary to existence." For Augustine there is no absolute ugliness but there is comparative deformity, objects which in comparison with others are less completely organized and symmetrical. Ugliness is the inverse of beauty, a privation of life. For Edmund Burke, the ugly partly coincided with the sublime, though not nearly so much as the beautiful from which nevertheless the sublime was distinguished.

Schlegel was the first to consider the ugly at length in an essay. Ugliness was for him "an unpleasant manifestation of the bad," a kind of negation of beauty. The ugly, Solger thought, is outside the beautiful and opposed to it. The ugly arises when the human mind finds in the commonplace something essential. Hegel denied the existence of an independent ugliness and put it in relation to man: ugliness proves to be a product of false characterization. For Croce the ugly is "unsuccessful expression," multiplicity instead of unity. The ugly can never be complete as the beautiful can, for if it were it would not be ugly; there is never the real presence of something which could be called "the ugly." Indeed Gilson claimed that bad art was art that had never achieved actual existence.

For Jordan the ugly like the beautiful is a principle and not a product; both ugly and beautiful are culture objects and can never be identified with anything actual, though they are evident in all aesthetic forms. In these terms ugliness is not a negative value, as Morris claimed, for its effects may be positive. We are repelled by the ugly because there is something positive at work in it as there is in any-

thing which has an effect, though we are not always repelled by the ugly art object, which sometimes exerts a kind
of fascination of its own. Of course neither the beautiful nor
the ugly is made so by human interest, as some have supposed (Jarrett, for instance). We are interested because
something is beautiful (or ugly), it is not beautiful (or ugly)
because we are interested.

Bad art may be of either one of two kinds: it may be what
is called "kitsch," or it may be the product of bad taste.

Kitsch is art that could be judged bad on the basis of the
criteria of any age, the result of substandard production, a
certain kind of art aimed at uninstructed mass appeal.
There is needless to add no cultivated version of kitsch.
Kitsch is art with its values dulled down, in effect the echoes
of genuine works of art which in another connection had
retained all of its sharp edges and its full power. Rodin is a
favorite kitsch sculptor because of the sentimentality of his
subject matter, but actually in a technical sense his work is
better than that. In the thousands of cheap and distorted
copies which are commercially produced and sold every
year, very little of his artistry remains and the sentiment is
thereby emphasized for all to see and feel. In an age of
emphasis on science most of the art which is popular is
kitsch art, and the fine arts have had to retreat to a position
of esoteric and eclectic appreciation by connoisseurs.

Kitsch has been studied, but bad art is not confined to
kitsch. There is also the kind which is the legitimate product of an age of bad taste, such as for instance the rococo
art much admired in 18th century France.

It is necessary to distinguish between bad art and the art
which deliberately employs the ugly for its aesthetic effect,
the qualitative counterpart of deliberately stated false

propositions. This is not bad art but great art which employs what for want of a better term we might designate as anti-beauty or, better still, counter-beauty. The art of counter-beauty achieves dazzling effects through the use of exaggeration, of contrasts and of suggested violence. It projects a mirror image of beauty and in this fashion suggests its overpowering quality. The most familiar examples may be seen in Mayan and Aztec sculpture and bas-relief—pre-Columbian art generally, and also in the gargoyles of the Gothic cathedrals in western Europe.

This is what Bosanquet called "difficult beauty" and what Stace described as "the unbeautiful." Morris considers the ugly as a species of beauty, and gives as examples "gargoyles, gruesome poetry, stark painting, and dissonant music." Certainly, the tendency to consider art as a kind of refinement has excluded some of the more powerful forms of beauty and some of the more grotesque varieties as well. But setting aside for the moment what is beautiful and what is ugly, the fact remains that generically speaking bad art is art just as much as good art is. We must not be led into assuming for example that bad poetry is not poetry. Such terms are not in themselves honorifics; they are names for specific classes. The unsuccessful painting is as much an example of the fine arts as the successful; both are generic works of art, for that is what the term means. It is a term of description, not one of judgment or evaluation.

What makes bad art bad? The definitions by themselves are not a sufficient guide; they do not enable us to decide in any given case whether a particular work of art is or is not bad art. Then, too, just to recognize the enormous complications, there is the case of art which is so bad, so very bad, that it can almost be considered good for that reason. An over-ornate and over-decorated sculpture might look quite good in a contemporary house which errs on the side of simplicity unless given the proper relief which such a work of art might provide. The complication arises from the neglected fact that art which is excellent in itself might show up badly against an inappropriate background. It would be possible to display a painting which is an unquestionable work of art against a background which might, temporarily at least, make it seem questionable.

It is possible, however, to consider the work of art independently of its environment. Having defined bad art, it now seems advisable to try to analyze the relations among the parts which account for the badness of bad art. These seem to sort themselves into a set of categories; eight, to be precise. Art is bad when (1) in a work of art the parts are more important than the whole; (2) when morality supercedes beauty; (3) when technique exceeds content; (4) when previous standards of the beautiful are employed in repetition; (5) when conventional evaluations are allowed to govern new work; (6) when pity replaces emotion; (7) when there is no organization or direction, and (8) when art is directed to ends other than the aesthetic.

1. *Art is bad when in a work of art the parts are more important than the whole.*

This is perhaps the archetypal example of bad art. In accordance with our definition of beauty, given at the outset, as the quality which emerges from the perfect bonding of parts in a whole, then, as we should expect, bad art results when in place of the perfect bonding the parts get out of hand and take over the whole, so that it becomes impossible to see the whole for the parts.

Most of the ambitious church architecture which is traditional in Europe exhibits features which can best be described as ugly and which therefore contribute to the total effect as bad art. The nondescript ground-plan of the Gothic cathedrals, their gratuitous decorations of parapets, of gargoyles, crestings and crockets, do nothing to enhance that unity of the whole which art requires. The sobbing degenerate end of this development is to be found finally not in the original stone, which the medieval cutters were so adept at shaping, but in the work of the jigsaw which enabled carpenters to embellish Victorian houses and even Mississippi River boats with the elaborate woodwork which has come to be known as "Steamboat Gothic."

But such faults are not limited to the Gothic. No better example presents itself than that of French Renaissance architecture for the over-decorated surface of its buildings, the lavish display of a profusion of rock-like forms (rococo, from French *rocaille* or rock-work) carved into scrolls, crimped shells and other elaborate shapes, all placed much too close together and set forth in an abundance of detail which could not help giving a total effect of confusion.

Only a practiced eye and a concentrated vision holding its attention on principles can see in some contemporary painting the same faults as those we have just noted in two of the chief traditional architectural styles in European cathedrals. An extreme example can be noted in certain contemporary paintings in which there is no whole except as indicated by the edges, there is only an assemblage of parts: some of the paintings of Pollock, some of Braque's still lifes, and the sculptures of David Smith. If art relies upon the perfect bonding of parts in a whole then that means, of course, their subordination to the whole. Art in which the parts themselves behave like wholes goes dead against the very meaning of art and therefore is singularly bad.

2. *Art is bad when morality supersedes beauty.*

Morality does supersede beauty when the work of art conveys a message in such a way that it stands before the aesthetic effects and has its impact independently of them. We have long had before us the examples of the medieval English morality plays and of *Pilgrim's Progress*. Harriet Beecher Stowe's *Uncle Tom's Cabin* was a notorious example, as was *Ramona* by Helen Hunt Jackson. The appalling condition of many of the Negro slaves on southern plantations and the equally appalling condition of the oppressed Indians were no doubt deserving of attention, and though these two novels may have had a good social effect in righting wrongs, that does not necessarily make for art in literature, as it assuredly did not do in either of these cases. Many of the novels produced in the Soviet Union during the Stalin regime and even after were designed primarily to advertise industrial progress in the socialist state. Indeed under the communist scheme of things, at least as interpreted by the masters of the Soviet Union and Communist China, every work of art must display as its first and more important meaning a political message intended to glorify the struggle of the working class, interpreted of course in party terms.

A variety of this kind of artistic error is exemplified when the moral message of a novel is improperly subordinated to the work as art and in addition assumes an undue prominence because the message itself conveys a false set of ideas. This is true of the novels of D. H. Lawrence for instance. That the primitive is stronger and more virile than the civilized, that blood thinks more vigorously than brain, that those who work closer to the soil are more intimately in touch with the true nature of things, are disguised fascist ideas parading as correctives of the over-preciosity of some of the more urban undertakings. Such concepts go against the facts, and when an artist as capable as Lawrence pursues them the result is to mar work which is otherwise excellent.

3. *Art is bad when technique exceeds content.*

This is apt to occur especially in an age of experimentation and innovation, but it may occur at other times as a result of fascination with complexities of technique. Most of the modern plastic arts are in this case. Abstract expressionism, when the subject has been eliminated altogether, or (since this is impossible) almost altogether, is a good example of the prominence of technique over content. Subject matter is of course content, and when it is eliminated the result is almost by definition bad art.

Bad art may occur as the result of fascination with complexities of technique. The composition of music because of its intricacies is peculiarly subject to the commission of this error. A few of the more complex of Bach's six part fugues which are dull in their overall effect do nothing to detract from the best of his work which stands with the greatest music of all time. Virtuosity as in the violin compositions of Wieniawski certainly belong with bad art. The virtuoso is concerned with performing dexterous feats on his instrument rather than with the art of music. The music of Antheil in the last generation, and of Cage and Stockhausen in this, are examples in point.

4. *Art is bad when previous standards of beauty are employed in repetition.*

The most familiar example is what is called academic

art, the art which imitates the discoveries made successfully by artists in the past. Academic art is never successful and that is why it is hard to give examples: they are not as a rule preserved. The neo-classic sculpture of the eighteenth century will serve, however, as will also the work of David, Piranesi and Canova, for instance, and the novels of William Dean Howells. Greek revival architecture which spread throughout Europe in the late eighteenth century was introduced into England in the nineteenth century and spread to Germany with the architect, Klemke. As a consequence of this revival almost every bank building in the United States as well as most southern plantation homes were imitations of the Greek temples of the classic period of Greek culture.

It is a sad and depressing thing to see new houses erected which are little more than cheap copies of what was once splendid examples of original architecture. New private dwellings which take their style from Greek temples, from Queen Anne and Georgian houses, and from French provincial farm houses, are not nearly so uncommon as from the aesthetic point of view they ought to be. Generally speaking, imitations are always second-rate. They follow the most superficial aspects of the forms while missing the power and the inner essence of the art they take as models. There is something empty, heavy-handed and dead about copies. It is not unusual for the copies to be done in cheaper and less durable materials than the originals; wood replaces stone, plaster replaces wood; in each instance a downgrading which gives ample evidence of the care and value placed upon the results.

But there have been entire cultures which exhibited in the main this imitative tendency. Roman culture, so able in political organization and in other areas, such as transportation, followed at secondhand the lead of the Greek artists. With the possible exception of the realism of the Roman portrait busts this seems to have been true of all the arts of the Romans, even including literature.

Virgil's *Bucolics* was a brazen borrowing from the *Idylls* of Theocritus, his *Aeneid* was fashioned after Homer's *Iliad* and *Odyssey*, and his *Georgics* came from Hesiod's *Works and Days*. Seneca owed much to Euripides. The subject matter of Ovid's *Metamorphoses* is the whole corpus of Greek mythology. *Lucretius' De Rerum Natura* was little more than a translation from a longer didactic poem by Epicurus. In a word, it can be said that so wide was the borrowing of the Roman from the Greek that Europe on the whole received its familiarity with Greek literature from Latin authors.

5. *Art is bad when conventional evaluations are allowed to govern new work.*

We have just considered the bad art which results from an imitation of style. Here the point is rather the imitation of method. Medieval tales were for the most part religious allegories. The influence of empiricism from the Renaissance onward has had a heavy effect upon the arts. Some of this influence has been good of course, but not all. In literature the close and literal interpretation of realism has reduced the novel to the level of good journalism. The novel of adventure was subtly transformed into the novel of vicarious experience. "You are there," the novelist now tells us; "you are seeing it happen almost as though it were happening to you." But where is the art in all this, and what values are evoked that will not date badly? Sinclair Lewis, it now appears, was more like a reporter who chose fiction as his medium.

"Science fiction" is a category invented for novels which undertake to extrapolate by imaginative means the experimental physical and biological sciences of the day. It worked very well when science was young, but now the advance of the sciences is so rapid that science fiction lags sadly behind science fact. Moreover the extrapolations the scientists themselves have made in terms of their sciences are so imaginative and—in older terms at least—so wild that the "science" of science fiction seems tame by comparison. The works of Jules Verne, for example, come under this limitation. *Around the World in Eighty Days* was a book that occasioned quite a stir when the trip took so many more days. But now it is possible to go around the world by jet in less than two days, and presumably with the supersonic aircraft now being built that time will be cut considerably.

To some extent no doubt all works of art must be governed in their construction by conventional evaluations. In a certain sense it is true that novels date if they are kept around long enough, and so it could fairly be claimed that all novels become historical novels. Yet the great artist invokes his own evaluations as well as his own new conceptions, and in this sense his work escapes the mark of history sufficient to remain as a perpetual value for successive generations because the values which it features do **not** "date" in that sense.

6. *Art is bad when pity replaces emotion.*

Much of the popular art of this or any day is devoted to the evocation of sentiments. The daytime "soap operas" of radio and television are of this character. Purgation through pity and terror it is not, however; nothing so strong as emotion, only such pity as entertainment can elicit. The "entertainment industry" would not survive in its present gigantic form were it to put a strain on its mass audience.

The appreciation of art is a great emotional gamble. For great art elevates, but bad art depresses; and there is usually in the world more bad art than great art. Sentiment is false emotion and leads to self-pity rather than to cosmic empathy or world-longing. Art elevates by lifting the individual above his petty concerns and into the struggle for values which exceed his own. It makes him a party to the values which stretch even beyond those of the human species, and which play some role in the composition of eternity. As Thomas Aquinas said, the individual's longing for the perpetual continuation of his being is one of his natural appetites, and we might add that it finds its best expression in great art.

But sentiment which parades as emotion of this sort is only disguised self-pity and so degrades the individual by reducing him to the level of his lowest concerns: the regret he feels for the fact that he must suffer a certain amount of anguish. The best examples of sentiment in art are perhaps to be found in an account of immediately popular novels, those which instantly reach a large audience but are forgotten in a very short time. From *In His Steps*, the novel which had in its day the highest sale of any in the United States, through *Anthony Adverse* to the recent example, *Love Story*, sentiment will be found to be the prevailing tone.

7. *Art is bad when there is no organization, no direction.*

A work of art must have a unity and a shape. This may

be apprehended all at once, as in an easel painting, or accumulated in time, as in a symphony or a novel. *Waiting for Godot* by Samuel Beckett was a deliberate attempt to leave such criteria behind and to allow the meaninglessness and lack of direction to tell its own story. Unfortunately, that was not sufficient, and the result is bad art. In painting the contemporary work of Francis Bacon and of Dubuffet achieve the same result. The fact that such conditions are deliberate does not make them any better. Recent French literature abounds with examples; the *nouvelles vagues*, novels without plot, and those novels which are printed without pagination on the theory that it does not matter what the order of the pages is, certainly illustrate the work of art that is without organization or direction. The paintings from the last period of Hans Hofmann, which he considered "Cézanne brought further" may be only Cézanne's geometry without the pictorial properties which Cézanne certainly held to assiduously, unless it is to be considered that whatever is encompassed within the limits of a rectangular canvas has an organization for that reason. The founder of abstract expressionism became its most revered victim.

8. *Art is bad when directed to ends other than the aesthetic.*

There is nothing wrong with putting works of art to other uses or with designing them with a view to reducing other needs provided the works are capable also of standing on their own as art. The most notable example is that of architecture. Most buildings with the possible exception of monuments are intended to be occupied, and were it not for that need they would not have been constructed. Yet they are at the same time works of art in themselves, and this is as true of the cathedral which was meant to be a house of worship as it is of the modern skyscraper which was constructed as an office building. Those European critics, like Sir Kenneth Clark, who admire the Gothic cathedral but refuse to see in the office skyscraper anything except its utilitarian value, are playing a safe game with the values of the past while steadfastly refusing to acknowledge those of the present and the future. The cathedral has a use also: it is used as a house of worship, without impairing or endangering its value as a work of art.

But when works of art are perverted to other uses at the expense of their own autonomous claims, then the result is genuinely bad art. This often happens when other interests are paramount; as for instance when low-cost housing and cheap constructions are concealed behind a pretentious facade of period architecture. The new methods of mass production are more influenced by such problems as ease of assembly, high profits, and popular and immediate appeal, than they are by aesthetic considerations.

Architecture is not the only offender in this kind of bad art. The cinema has been equally guilty. Here sheer size has been the ideal. The "super-colossal" productions in which thousands of men and horses have participated, such as *Ben Hur, The Ten Commandments* and *Cleopatra* are veritable monuments to bad art. Size, sheer size, long films, loud noises, all mistaken to be indications of achievement, employing at the same time representations of sentiment and brutality intended to stagger rather than elevate, are in our time the clearest expressions of this kind of bad art.

A familiar variety of art which is bad because it is directed to other ends is the art which serves subordinately in another art. The literary description in paintings, so much

liked in the eighteenth century, such as the canvases of
Greuze in which literary values substituted for pictorial
values which were scarcely present at all, and the vogue for
"respectable" imitations of classic Greek art which were so
common in the nineteenth century are obvious examples. As
late as the early twentieth century the California coast was
dotted with the "ruins" of classic Greek architecture made
of painted *papier mache* laid over chicken wire, themselves
falling into ruins. The romantic appeal of classic ruins,
whether conveyed in poetry or in painting takes art out of
its proper sphere and into that of special pleading for a lost
culture. Bouguereau and Cabanel, Leighton and Poynter
are splendid examples of painters who introduced elements
from a domain where other values prevailed.

The overwhelming effects of bad art has not been sufficiently recognized. Its importance is due to its prevalence:
there is in the world quantitatively speaking more bad art
than good. This is true as of now; whether it was true also
in periods of great taste, such as fifth century Athens, is
another question. We do not have the evidence necessary to
judge for we do not have everything that was done in that
period. But in many other periods the case is easier to make
out; and since the rise of the great populations, since the
eighteenth century, say, the preponderance of bad art over
good must go unquestioned. The mass arts cater to the
masses who by definition are uncultivated yet whose
judgment prevails. The cultural elite, however instructed,
are dictated to by the artists who judge themselves to be the
true criteria of what constitutes good art since they must
produce it. They give their public what they think it should
have, and what it eventually will want. But the artists who
cater to the masses through the popular arts in the "world

of entertainment" give the masses what they think the masses want at the time. And while the masses are fickle, there are great rewards to be gathered in the meanwhile. When art is judged good by the elite it is apt to remain indefinitely, but whether the popular arts are judged good or bad they are destined not to be around very long. On democratic grounds everyone should be free to produce what he wishes for whatever reason, and to cultivate what he likes however good or bad it may be. But the evaluations which long periods of time make possible to generations of cultivated people are apt to be on the side of good art whether produced for the elite or for the masses. And so it is a service to be able to be able to discriminate somewhat in advance by preselecting good art wherever and whenever possible.

In an age of large populations, which is also an age of mass productions, we are under the necessity of learning to live with a man-made environment which is predominantly ugly. Not only is the environment polluted in physical and chemical ways which makes it biologically unsuitable, it is also polluted aesthetically, and this while perhaps less immediately dangerous does have its deleterious effects. For the environment of urban populations and even of farm communities in industrial countries is chiefly an ugly one, and so perhaps without anyone being aware of it this factor serves to increase the mood of discontent and dissatisfaction. Not all of such unhappiness stems from ways we do not like; much of it comes from the sheer ugliness of our surroundings.

FOURTEEN

The Aesthete

The dilettante is one who professionally engages in an activity merely for his own amusement. When for an individual that activity is connected with art in some way other than its origination and comprises his chief preoccupation, we have the spectacle of the aesthete. Usually though not always the aesthete is an art collector. The aesthete belongs to that species of dilettante with greater pretensions than the others, for he presumes to a higher degree of sensitivity to beauty. And while he includes the beauties of nature in that category, he is especially concerned with the beauty of the fine arts.

In the great centers of civilization there are always social groups which revolve around the appreciation of the arts. Their members are rich and cultivated and endowed with leisure, and have no stronger ambition than to live beautifully among beautiful things. By definition seldom are ambitious men found in such groups. They are populated rather by those with no wider aims than can be comprised by aesthetic enjoyment. Although art is the dominant theme, originative artists are seldom members for they are more ambitious. One is more likely to find there art critics, art patrons, museum directors, although needless to add not all of these are aesthetes in the sense defined. It is hard to get rid of the notion that a faint odor of patchouli pervades the delicate and precious atmosphere in which the aesthetes live exquisitely among their treasures.

Now admittedly, to produce and appreciate art is a sign of high civilization, and a condition toward which all cultivated people aspire. But somehow something is wrong. What it is and what one could do to correct it is the topic of the present inquiry.

To understand a little better what is involved, it may be necessary to look more closely at the nature of works of art. These call upon different capacities in those who produce them and those who merely enjoy them.

The production of art is an active affair, while the appreciation of art is passive. The artist is an active searcher, and moreover one who is engaged in a ceaseless battle to impose his aesthetic sensibilities through his will upon what must be to a large extent at least intractable material. All is not beauty in his world, beauty is only the result of his effort to express the truth of feelings in material terms, and to this end to meet and overcome the resistance which stone or clay or sounds offer. He is engaged in a monumental contest with powerful forces, and if he is victorious he produces a work of art.

Compare this picture of a life-pattern with that of the

aesthete, whom we might define as the professional appreciator of works of art. His is a wholly passive assignment, and this in a world of active striving is debilitating at best. His ambition is merely to expose himself to works of art or if he can to buy and accumulate them and so to surround himself with beautiful things, and this is true of the decorative arts as well as the fine arts. The aesthete receives, he does not give. His is the assignment of self-cultivation without contrast. If possible he banishes from the immediate environment anything which might disturb the perfection of his milieu, which is one of beauty and nothing but beauty.

There is a cross-breed type, the artist-aesthete or aesthete-artist, partaking of both aesthete and artist. A supreme example, perhaps, is Jean Cocteau, a showman who was both aesthete and artist by turns, an actor who always played himself first and foremost. It is too early to say whether his artistic works, his poems, plays, novels and sculpture will survive. If they do then the artist in him has prevailed over the aesthete; but if they do not, then the aesthete will have prevailed over the artist. He differed from the artist in thinking fame more important that the production of works of art, and he differed from the aesthete in being productive.

The aesthete, when he can afford to be one, is a collector. He is usually more concerned, however, with collecting the art done in the past than with that done in the present. Classic art is apt to be a selection, a distillation, of the best; and such a process has not yet had the time to make a separation in contemporary art. Much more discrimination is required if one is to pick one's way among contemporary works to make a good collection than to acquire what is already time-tested. Classic art, with that patina which long endurance lends to everything except organisms, seems less crude by comparison with the fresh work of contemporaries.

Then, too, there is no necessity under such a program to come into contact with living artists. Artists as persons are usually rougher than aesthetes; they have more power, and the expression of power, and especially of its by-products, is apt to be something less than polished. As Nietzsche observed in *Thus Spake Zarathustra*, "it is necessary to have chaos within one in order to give birth to a dancing star." There is as much difference in vigor between the artist and the aesthete as there is between the English novelist and the English scholar. Their aims are diverse, and the success of the one is a challenge to the other.

The aesthete relies upon greatness by association. He somehow feels that he has fulfilled his mission as a person if he has continually and exclusively exposed himself to the influence of works of art which were produced by men whose sensibilities exceeded his own. In his way he is able to identify himself through the appreciation of great art with the great artists and subsequently feels himself entitled to be one of their company, in spirit if not in practice. This is a syllogism from the logic of actual events, whose premises are true but whose conclusion surprisingly enough is false, and this is made possible because the inference does not hold, for from the premises no such conclusion follows. It is simply not true that because a man has made a practice of appreciating the work of others he is in any way therefore the equal of those others. A cat can look at a king, it has been said, but that does not endow the cat with any regal stature.

If a work of art commands respect it is because it has connections which extend not only to the aesthete but in many other directions. The work of art is a material object which has been altered through human agency with a view to intensifying its effects on those whose senses disclose its value to them. It can only do this through its connections with material objects, whose proportions have been changed in such a way that its qualities can be more readily encountered. What gives an object the value it has is how it organizes the effects of all its connections. Thus art consists in symbols somehow standing for true values—in a word, little representations of larger segments of the actual world. To confine its effects to the aesthete would be possible only if it were smaller than it is.[1] The aesthete by his very sense of possessiveness and exclusivity threatens art appreciation even if not the value of the art itself. If the work in question is great it stands for values which contradict his very professional existence.

But perhaps the most glaring difference between the artist and the aesthete is the difference of aims. The artist is an objectivist; he wishes to change in the world something which he thinks he can improve through his labors. He cares nothing for himself but is wholly devoted to the work of art: it exists where nothing like it existed before. He is content if he has added to the beauty of the world by making a work of art. The aesthete, on the other hand, is a subjectivist; he wishes to take as much from the world as is necessary in order to surround himself with the kind of environment his nature requires. He cares only for himself and is utterly devoted to self-cultivation. He wishes to live a

[1] Cf. the excellent statement by Bertram Morris, *The Aesthetic Process* (Evanston, Illinois 1943, Northwestern University), p. 31.

beautiful life but succeeds only in living a life surrounded by beauty, a life which in itself is not always so beautiful.

There is an important distinction then, between the aesthete and the artist, and one which has to be recognized. But if the aesthete is no artist, neither is he a connoisseur or an art historian. The professional connoisseur, like the art historian, cultivates an important area, and the distinction here is a difficult one to make; nevertheless it must be made. The difference hangs on an attitude not only toward art but toward the world, an exclusivity which shuts out the rest of the world for the aesthete but does not do so for the connoisseur. The art historian is in no position professionally to be so exclusive, for the history of art is intimately connected with the history of human culture and of civilization generally. The art of a period would seem to represent the culture of that period, so that to an aesthete a particular art is a distillation of experience; the art of ancient Greece for instance, of medieval China or of Renaissance Italy. This is to some extent true, yet it has its limitations. For in such a program of appreciation there are omitted elements: the color and vigor of life, the contradictions and conflicts, the struggles and failures.

The aesthete has to be distinguished from the bohemian. The bohemian is not a true snob but only a counter-snob. The counter-snobbery of those art lovers who dress in drab and tattered clothes and who look down on the rich and advantaged from the alleged heights of a superior sensibility are not the true aesthetes though easily mistaken for them. The deliberately rude manners and the ostentatious lack of possessions of those who claim an affinity with the arts above those who are in a position to possess them may be listed as a sort of corollary group to the aesthetes but they do not belong with them properly speaking. They do not live in art but only at its borders and they do not pursue beauty as assiduously. It should not be necessary to add that the bohemian is not an artist, either; he shares that lack with the aesthete.

The aesthete is once removed from actual life. The early world before the artist first appeared in it contained both cooperation and competition, and that same ambivalence of aggression which compels animals to hurt as well as help their own species still prevails throughout the inorganic world. In biology, from symbiosis to the food chain; in astronomy, from solar systems to colliding galaxies, the same ambivalence of directions and of interactions is to be found. Art, on the other hand, reads all phenomena harmoniously, which is only half the story for in works of art even wars are painted as though they were tableaux in which no one really got hurt. Art is a record only of successes and only of artistic successes at that. It is no substitute for the immediate experience of life in all of its force and with its myriad of detail. Life is a whole, and art is only a part of that whole, however admirable and preferable a part.

The aesthete solves this problem in an unique manner. He undertakes to avoid the roughness of life by choosing to live altogether in an artificial environment and at the same time to shun specific human failings. To avoid contradiction, the artificial environment must be entirely a product of men of genius. Nature in its non-human phase, nature untouched by human efforts, is altogether too crude and vulgar for the aesthete. Nature is monotonous; nature is obvious. The variety and subtlety sought by the aesthete is to be found only in works of art. The aim is not limited to works of fine art but could be extended to the botanical world.

Parks and gardens extending beyond houses sufficiently to shield the owner from all contact with the vulgar condition of nature in its native state, is what the aesthete seeks.

Such a life has one serious limitation, one occasioned by the fact that art has meaning without reference. When we know what a work of art means, we still do not know to what it refers; the reference has long ago disappeared in most cases and only the meaning has remained. This gives it a curious sort of abstract quality. And however elevating and even intoxicating art may be, however essential to a cultivated existence it must be, it still will not serve as a substitute for immersion in the actual striving which is the way of life for most of those who labor under the necessity of earning a living.

Living on art alone, which is what the aesthete undertakes to do, is like living on alcohol alone, it provides food for the spirit and somehow gives the feeling of nourishment while lacking in vitamins. The alcoholic suffers in the end not from his periods of mood elevation but rather from the lack of essential elements in his diet, with the result that he dies from some one or a combination of the deficiency diseases. The aesthete has had enough cake, but he has not had enough protein. He becomes spiritually pale and anemic and if he does not die exactly, he at least becomes weak and breathless.

As so many philosophers have thought in the past— Schopenhauer, for instance—art is an escape from ordinary life and a relief from the innumerable pressures of daily living, from the struggle for existence in which man no less than the other species is engaged. It is an escape into the worlds of things-as-they-could-be, including the world of things-as-they-ought-to-be, the world as contrary-to-fact. It is an escape, but not a substitute; and it cannot function as a substitute. A life lived entirely in terms of art, a life surrounded by beauty and the beautiful, is a life without contrast. It misses the sharp comparison which lends to both art and life some of their values.

For the fact is that art does not provide a full environment for man, however valuable an ingredient it may be, and this lack operates both ways. The aesthete is not of the stuff of which an art is made, and art does not offer the variety of products of which a man is made. Life at times may seem to imitate art, but the fact is that life is more complex and offers many more aspects than the one that art has selected. Art offers intensity, it does not offer completeness; only life offers that. The world is more dense with properties than any of our devices have succeeded in screening out, and art is only one of those devices.

It is well known that the same work of art can mean different things to different people. The value of a given work of fine art is probably more than can be elicited by any one person. To some extent at least the appreciation of a work of art depends not only on the value of the art itself—that goes without saying—but also on the equipment which the appreciator brings to the experience. What he derives from an experience depends as much on what he is equipped to derive from it as on what there is in it to be derived. Presumably, a man with immense and varied experience in the world who yet has the requisite sensibilities can get more out of a work of art than one who has the latter equipment but not the former. The aesthete is a case in point. He may have deepened his sensibilities with prolonged exposure to works of fine art, but he may lack the varied and non-artistic experience which would enable him to see it in the round, so to speak. Specialization has its limitations, and those of the aesthete are painfully apparent.

How the aesthete endeavors to substitute art for life is amply illustrated by Des Esseintes in Huysmans' *A Rebours.* The merely sensuous aesthete seldom reaches the essence of art but is apt to concentrate on its borders, where he finds attenuated manners and styles. He learns about periods in art, about its peculiarities, but seldom feels the impact of its power. With the aesthete is introduced a kind of preciosity and pedantry which is actually misleading to art appreciation, as misleading as the scholar's preoccupation with it often is. In the aesthete's world art exists "for art's sake," and he recoils from the thought that art might be anything so practical as "the education of the senses," a by-product of purely emotional enjoyment. Use he regards as adulteration, and no less so when it is an aesthetic use than when it is an ethical one.

Art in its proper proportions is necessary to a full life, which is, however, bigger than art. It functions to make us feel what external reality is like, a reality which is so much bigger and more complex than we are, and capable therefore of a greater degree of intensity. Yet it cannot do this if we remain forever inside the arts. Des Esseintes to the contrary notwithstanding, opening a window ought to provide immediate contact with the activity of the hurly-burly world, not with the passive beauty of a polychrome easel painting.[2] What has been called in the study of space environments "cabin ecology" can offer at best only a temporary refuge.

The aesthete, on the other hand, lives in a conveniently

[2] J. -K. Huysmans, *A Rebours.*

arranged isolated segment of the world surrounded by a vacuum, so far as he can manage it. Into this ecological community little outside interference is allowed to penetrate. It is a self-contained system: he takes care of his art treasures, they respond by furnishing to him all of the spiritual warmth of which he stands in need.

The aesthete is a votary of art, and his occupational disease comes from taking art too seriously and even solemnly. Moreover, the man who spends all of his time in art appreciation misses the innermost essence of art itself, being too much exposed to its externals and yet lacking the proper contrast. He is like that religious man who spends so much time performing the rituals that he never quite reaches the belief, because the faith which he takes so much for granted stands in his way.

Art enhances life but not when it is used as a substitute for life. The appreciation of art elevates when it accompanies living and the struggle toward some non-artistic goal; it depresses when it substitutes for life and damps down the struggle. Those who carry along with them an appreciation of the arts while engaged in the struggle for something else will find that art deepens and enriches existence. But where the appreciation of art is employed as a substitute, as it is with either the aesthete, the connoisseur or the dilettante, then its effect is to cheapen, and it becomes a very superficial affair.

The typical aesthete is without responsibilities of any sort. Usually he has no wife, and almost never any children. He supports nobody, deeming it a sufficient social contact if he himself is supported. He prepares himself for his wholehearted dedication to art appreciation by having as few ties and as little demands on his time as possible. His devotion to art is overwhelming, his absorption in his own cultivation supreme. He needs to give nothing for what he has been given, only to take and use, claiming for justification only that what he enjoys is a superior product and his own enjoyment of it clear evidence of his own superiority.

The aesthete tends to be a social snob. He looks up to men of wealth or family and seeks to identify himself with them. Correspondingly, he entertains an overbearing attitude toward those he believes to be below him in the social scale. Even the artistocrat sometimes can be looked down on by the art collector who is, in his own estimation, of the highest rank because of his taste and sensibilities. Acton thought that the Irish aristocracy were lowly folk who engaged in sport but had redeemed themselves in the past when some of them had been collectors of painting and patrons of architecture.[3]

The snobbish disdain is not restricted to those with lesser interests and activities; it is extended even to research scientists. Santayana, for instance, referred to the physicists as inventors (I am inclined to think he knew better but intended a gratuitous insult). "If we ask the inventors what they have learned of the depths of nature, which sometimes they have probed with such astonishing success, their faces remain blank. They may be chewing gum. . . ."[4] Santayana himself, it may be noted, was an aesthete as well as a philosopher.

Only a society in which leisure is possible can provide the conditions favorable to the aesthete. The soil most favorable

[3] Harold Acton, *Memoirs of An Aesthete* (New York, 1970, Viking Press), p. 271.
[4] George Santayana, *Some Turns of Thought in Modern Philosophy* (New York 1933, Scribner's), p. 71.

to his growth is the inheritance of sufficient capital to render the earning of a living unnecessary. Poor aesthetes have been known to occur, though more rarely. The aesthete need not be an art collector, though he usually is. For to be an aesthete essentially means to have a certain attitude toward life rather than to do a certain thing about it. The attitude involves self-cultivation based on the cult of beauty.

The aesthete need not be an art collector, but it is also true that the art collector need not be an aesthete. Some rich men who have made great fortunes buy paintings and sculpture for themselves simply because they love art, or it may be that they buy art in the same way they buy diamonds and emeralds for their wives, as a way of displaying their commercial success. These men in any case tend not to be aesthetes, though their sons may be.

There are such things as professional preoccupations. Civilization is so complex and so specialized that it is all anyone can do to know his own field well. A man who had made himself thoroughly acquainted with a single art or even with the art of a particular period has had his hands full. But this is true of the art critic, and the aesthete does not set himself up as an art critic even though at times his knowledge may be equal to the challenge. The professional preoccupation of the aesthete is nothing so useful to others; it consists in his relation to the arts and almost to the arts alone. He does not have an unselfish dedication, such as the artist may have, but on the contrary quite a selfish one.

Art, in a word, may be what we live by; it cannot be what we live for. There is a deep need in man, the animal, for the common prosaic things, and a continual urgency exists within most of us to change the world, hopefully for the better. This always has its ugly side, since war is not the only kind of competition, but the ugly makes a needed contrast with the beautiful, and art, however necessary, by its very nature will always have to be something special.

Index

Index

Index

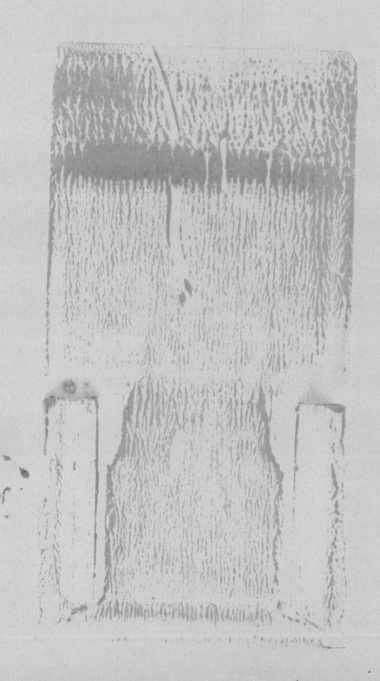